Changing India

Insights from the Margin

Changing India
Insights from the Margin

ROBIN THOMSON

B.R. Publishing Corporation
[A Division of BRPC (India) Ltd.]
Delhi-110035

Distributed by :
BRPC (India) Ltd.
4222/1, Ansari Road, Darya Ganj,
New Delhi-110002
Ph. : 3259196, 3259648
Fax : 3201571
E-Mail : *brpcltd@del2.vsnl.net.in*

© 2002 Robin Thomson (b. 1943—)

ISBN 81-7646-292-6

Published by :
B. R. Publishing Corporation
[A Division of BRPC (India) Ltd.]
3779, 1st Floor, Kanhaiya Nagar,
Tri Nagar, Delhi-110035
E-Mail: *brpcltd@del2.vsnl.net.in*

Laser Typeset by :
Raj Kumar
Delhi-110 035

Printed at :
Chawla Offset Printers,
Delhi-110052

PRINTED IN INDIA

For Shoko

For Shoko

Acknowledgements

This book is based on other people's work. So my thanks
go first of all to those friends who have allowed me to tell a
little of their stories here. They have inspired and taught me.
The facts I have written are accurate, I hope. The
interpretations and comments are based entirely on my own
perspectives.

I'm also grateful to many other friends and colleagues
who are not mentioned. They live in India or the Diaspora
and come from various faith backgrounds. I'm so glad to
have them as friends.

Jay and Anita Bhattacharjee, Probir and Binoo Sen, and
their families, have been close friends since student days.
This book is really for them.

Special thanks to Raju Abraham, Bimal Krishna Das,
Ram Gidoomal, Prabhu Guptara, Deepak Mahtani, Vishal
Mangalwadi, David Porter, Sarah Thomson and Jonathan
Thomson, who have read various drafts and given constant
encouragement and careful comments.

In chapters 6, 7 and 8 I have made extensive use of
material by Katherine Makower, Beulah Wood and Joy
Pachuau (on Ashirvad, Iris Paul and the North East) to
supplement my own meetings and visits.

This is not an academic book and so there are no
footnotes. But you will find at the back a list of the books
quoted and some others that have been helpful. Where

quotations are included in the text from books in that list, they are referenced to the list by author and year of publication. Other references, where provided, are included in the body of the text.

Robin Thomson

Foreword

Reading this book, I have a strong sense of deja-vu. I recognise this account of returning to an India much changed, because that has been my experience also.

My family comes from Hyderabad Sind in northern India, a region that is now part of Pakistan. After Partition my family had to move to East Africa, where I was born in 1950. Our family never forgot India and spoke of it constantly. I was brought up with such a familiarity with my mother country that I could probably have directed you round Indian towns I had never visited.

In the late 1960s when Kenya gained Independence we became refugees for a second time. In 1967 I arrived with my family in London.

By 1988 I was an executive working for an international corporation: my work gave me the opportunity to visit my mother country. I took with me my own notion of India, gained from other people's memories, but could hardly recognise it in the India to which I came. The old palaces had mostly become hotels, the influence of Western culture was evident on every hand, and many old traditions had given way to a modernised way of doing things. Most striking of all, the gap between India's rich and India's poor had widened. The experience of being shown around the slums of Mumbai, said to be the worst in Asia, changed my life. In recent years I have visited India again, this time as a

business consultant. Once again I found that India had
changed dramatically. It is not long ago that telephones were
few and far between once you moved out of the main urban
areas. Now, due almost wholly to the work of
telecommunications visionary Sam Pitroda, a telephone is
within reach of every Indian – and mobile phones are to be
seen in plenty.

It is about this country – indeed, this sub-continent – that
has seen so many changes, that Robin Thomson has written
this book. I am glad that he makes the important point that
despite the current political problems surrounding religious
conversion, India's rich heritage of pluralism and tolerance
is by no means unfriendly towards religious diversity. As one
who has become a *chela* (disciple) of the *Sanatana Sat Guru
Yesu Masih* (the Lord Jesus Christ), I am grateful to my
family for the ethical values and standards that the Hindu
faith commends and which I inherited. For example, the
principle of *Dharma* (Duty) to family, extended family and
community, and many other aspects that give me the best of
all traditions that I embrace. The book centres on the theme
of conversion. Robin asks some searching questions, which
I think can be summarised in the question, 'When faith
changes, is that all that changes?' He presents some
fascinating portraits of individuals who are changing the face
of India for the better – doctors, teachers, artists,
entrepreneurs and many more – and discovers that conversion
was a factor in their motivation.

The question with which he begins – How can India be
changed for the better? – is one that all Indians (living in
India or the Diaspora) who care for our great and ancient
nation, must consider. The challenge that his book presents
is to regard religious conversion, whatever our own faith, as
a factor to be acknowledged in social revolution: and in so

doing, to acknowledge that India's historic tolerance and pluralist climate of ideas is therefore a particularly fertile seedbed for change. India has nothing to fear from genuine religious converts, or indeed from genuine missionary enterprise: on the contrary, there is much to be gained. This is a book for all who care about India's future and her spiritual and physical well-being.

Ram Gidoomal*

---

* ***Ram Gidoomal*** *was awarded the CBE for services to the Asian community and to race relations in the UK. He was a candidate in the 2000 London Mayoral election, supported by Asian business and religious leaders. He is Chairman of South Asian Development Partnership as well as board member or advisor to numerous businesses and government bodies.*

Contents

Introduction

The philosophers have tried to understand India.
The point is to change it.
(with apologies to Karl Marx)

Throughout the twentieth century, every one of India's leaders followed Marx's advice (misquoted above). From Vivekananda to Vajpayee, from Mahatma Gandhi to the Nehru-Gandhis, they have all been in the business of trying to change India for the better.

Of course Gandhiji would not have agreed that understanding is unnecessary. How could you change India without understanding her deep traditions, her rich cultural diversity and the ancient wisdom of her people (interpreted by Gandhiji's inner voice)? To do him justice, Karl Marx also believed that understanding was important. Communism, his programme for change, was based on a profound analysis of why the world is as it is.

That analysis was one of the many influences on Jawaharlal Nehru, who wanted to change India into an egalitarian, democratic, socialist state. For Indira Gandhi it was *Garibi hatao* ('away with poverty') and the Twenty-Point Programme. For Rajiv Gandhi education, technology and computers were going to bring the transformation.

The point that everybody recognises is not *whether* to change India, but *how*, and in what direction?

Should we go back to the past, to India's ancient

wisdom? A chorus of voices calls us in that direction. Or does India's destiny lie in the future, with her scientists and technologists? Will Bangalore become the software capital of the world?

Might it be possible for India to keep the past and the future together – the bullock-cart, the Maruti and the space vehicle *(Aryabhata)* side by side? Could that mean that the peace and stability of the villages will temper the rush and dynamic of the cities, in a satisfying harmony? Or will it just mean that grinding poverty continues, alongside conspicuous wealth?

Who will be the agents of change? The politicians, as they would like us to think? Or the journalists, the industrialists, the artists, the business people, the film-makers, the film-stars, the Naxalites, the environmentalists, the teachers, the children, the social workers, the Internet whiz-kids, the scholars, the saints, the god-men, the missionaries ...?

I don't claim to understand India or to know in which direction she should change. But India has been a part of me – or rather, I have been a part of India – since I was born 6,000 feet up in the Himalayas in Mussoorie, north of Delhi. My parents had come to work in India; they met in the Mussoorie Hindi language school. My sister, brother and I were all born in Uttar Pradesh, India's biggest state, which, if it were a separate country, would be the world's eighth most populous nation. We began our schooling in the Nilgiris, another mountain range in South India, and continued it in Britain.

I arrived back in India in 1966 to work, straight from university.

Like everybody else, I wanted to do my bit in the changing India. I had definite ideas. I wanted to see people with clean water, hunger removed, the poverty gap closed, good health care and self-sufficiency in food. In those days people talked about the economy 'taking off', and everybody hoped that it would.

But I didn't know how I could contribute to all that. I was a missionary.

A missionary? India has seen plenty of those over the last 2,500 years. Buddhist, Jain, Hindu (both inside and outside India), Muslim, Christian ... India has both received and exported missionaries. Did any of them make a difference?

I wasn't even a missionary with useful qualifications, like a doctor, educator or agriculturalist. My subject was the Bible and theology, and I had come to teach it to others. What use was that, in the face of India's needs? How could I contribute to India, let alone bring change?

In the thirty-five years that have passed since then, India *has* changed profoundly. And I have learned a few things and made a lot of friends all over India, which is one of the privileges of being a teacher. I have seen them at work and have observed what they are contributing to India's transformation. In this book I want to share some of their stories, to try to learn what kind of contribution can help to transform India.

I want to try to answer another question as well. Missionaries have always been enigmatic people – slightly odd, occasionally comical, sometimes sinister. On the whole they have been seen as benign, doing good in their own way, however irrelevant that might be to the 'real' issues of development and economic progress. The 'missionary spirit' was synonymous with commitment and dedication. But some have always disliked them and suspected their motives. Even Gandhiji expressed himself with some acerbity on the subject of Christian missionaries:

If instead of confining themselves purely to humanitarian work such as education, medical services to the poor and the like, they would use these activities of theirs for the purpose of proselytising, I would certainly like them to withdraw. Every nation considers its own faith to be as good as that of any other. Certainly the great faiths held by the people of India are adequate for her people. India stands in no need of conversion from one faith to another.

From time to time that feeling has become general and missionaries have become the target of hostility. It has not happened very often, because of India's astonishing tolerance and willingness to let all kinds of weeds grow side by side in the garden. But at the present time, at the beginning of the twenty-first century, a lot of questions are being asked about 'missionary activity'. Does it destroy culture? In particular, what is the place of 'conversion' in missionaries' work? What does conversion mean? How does it relate to the 'good works' done by many missionaries? Are they a cover-up? An inducement? Are they just a means to an end – conversion, exploitation, de-culturisation ...?

Is there a place for religious conversion in the modern world?

There are actually very few foreign missionaries in India today. But some see the Indian church and Indian missionaries as mere extensions of foreign agencies, and so the suspicion continues. Influential journalists, business people and politicians have taken this view. What is the truth? As I have wrestled with these questions, I have found myself turning again to my friends and their work for answers.

Judge for yourself. In the pages that follow you will find their stories, along with my reflections, comments, questions and sometimes arguments – insights from the margin.

1
Coming Home:
India in the Sixties

Venkataswami Gupta was the son of a moneylender, born into a Chettiar family in Cuddapah District of Andhra Pradesh. Money and business were in his blood.

At the age of eighteen his life was turned around. It began with his own failure. His father wanted him to become a lawyer and continue the family business. He sent him to a school in a nearby town and made sure that he had plenty of pocket money. Venkat wasted the money and failed all his exams that year. Furious, his father brought him home and stopped all his allowances.

In business families like the Guptas, nobody is trusted to handle money except family members. In their shops or offices an assistant may serve the customers, but there is always a family member at the cash box. Venkat couldn't even fulfil this trust. His hand was soon dipping into the till to finance his pleasures. Frustrated, he knew that he was doing wrong but couldn't help it. When his aunt gave him a copy of the *Bhagavad Gita* to read, its high ethical standards seemed to confirm what he already knew. His behaviour was condemned and he needed to change his ways – but he didn't know how to.

One day he heard, outside his house, preachers with a revolutionary message that offered him a way out of his dilemma. His life was changed and he began to preach this message enthusiastically to others. His family, however, were not pleased at this. They cut him off completely. He became a travelling preacher and eventually started a college in Madras to train others as preachers.

In 1966 I was in my final year at university in England. My father who was still working in India heard about the college and discovered that they were looking for staff. He suggested that I should teach there for a year or two. I knew very little of what that might involve, but it seemed a good learning experience. So I decided to go for two years, expecting to return to England after that. The cheapest way to travel was by a French ship, MV Laos, sailing from Marseilles to Yokohama via Bombay and Colombo. The eleven-day journey cost £100 including the train fare from London. I was in the *Classe Cabine*, which sounded better than *Economy Class* but in reality included three-quarters of the ship's passengers, crowded into one quarter of the ship's space. We were a varied group: Indians returning from holiday or study, Arabs bound for Aden, Europeans going to India for adventure, pilgrimage or work (I seemed to be the only one in this last category), and a sizeable contingent of Japanese. One of them, Shoko, had also been studying theology, in London.

On Sunday 18 September 1966, we arrived in India. The ship docked at Bombay near the famous Gateway of India. After a bruising encounter with the Customs over typewriters I had brought for the college, I transferred my luggage to the

Bombay-Madras Mail. Thirty-two hours later I arrived back in Madras, where I had lived as an eleven-year old, to teach in the college established by Venkataswami (now Dr) Gupta.

Madras, 1966

Soft crispy dosais, fluffy white iddlis, crunchy vadais, with hot sambar or coconut chutney.

A sprawling, old-fashioned city of broad shady avenues, crowded shopping streets and winding alleys. Large colonial bungalows in spreading shady compounds. The oriental splendour of Moor Market alongside the classical elegance of the Corporation's Ripon Building. Central Station, Fort St George and Spencer's. Untidy construction everywhere, with piles of bricks and sand and crazy wooden scaffolding. Slums springing up, with thatched huts, muddy paths and open drains. The thirteen-storey LIC Building, sticking up like a sore thumb over the city. Government offices with piles of dusty files, clerks bent over their work or sleeping under the slowly turning fans, peons guarding their officers' doors. Girls walking to school with fresh flowers in their hair. Brightly painted temples with blaring loudspeakers. Cycle rickshaws, buses, handcarts, cars, taxis, scooters, cycles, people. Piles of rubbish at street corners. Huge cinema hoardings with giant film stars. A vast lunch at the prestigious Dasaprakash Hotel for Rs 1.25 (Madras Meals) or Rs 1.50 (Bombay Meals – more chapatis, different flavours). The rise of the DMK (Dravida Munnetra Kazhagam), with their 'rising sun' image plastered everywhere. Hot humid weather all year round. Graceful coconut palms, spiky palmyras. Mount Road and the Marina Beach; white sand stretching for forty kilometres. Coca Cola and fresh coconut water, both available for the same price. Saturday mornings at the vast Corporation swimming pool,

*with its stinging chlorinated water. The all-pervasive smell
of the sea, dried fish and the smelly Cooum River. Smiling,
friendly faces.*

Coming home.

Chennai, 1999

*Colossal new buildings of marble, glass and steel,
towering apartment blocks, gleaming shopping malls. Eleven
new flyovers in construction. Whole new cities of well
ordered suburban 'colonies'. Acres of slums and Slum
Clearance Housing Colonies. Dense traffic, choking
pollution. Twenty-nine TV channels. Whirlpool washing
machines, Internet cafés, Video CDs. Domino's Pizza. A
gaping, ugly car park in place of Moor Market. The return
of the DMK, with their 'rising sun' image plastered
everywhere. Smiling, friendly faces.*

Home again.

India in the 1960s

I was back in India. But what was I going to do? The
reality of India rose up and hit me, as I stared out of the train
window on the long journey from Bombay to Madras: 450
million people, so diverse, so full of contrasts, such rich
resources, such apparent needs. Where did I begin? What
should I do? Were there any solutions? What were the real
questions? I had come to teach, but what was my message?

I was sharing a compartment with a young sales
executive, T. K Shetty, who gave me his pithy opinions on
the current scene. After arriving in Madras I travelled further
south with my father to Madurai, where my parents were
working. It was a day's journey by train and we had plenty
of time to talk. My father was matter-of-fact about the issues.
I knew that he loved India passionately and had many close

friends. They welcomed me into their families too, as I tried to absorb the new situation.

In 1966 India had just come through the Bihar famine. Thousands had died of starvation. Food was still being imported, and mountains of PL480 wheat and rice stood at the quaysides. Some of it had proved to be sub-standard and had been left to rot. The 'Green Revolution' that transformed India's agriculture in the 1970s was still in the future.

Most people's predictions were gloomy: continuing dependence, exploding population. A few looked wistfully back to the colonial order. Many more wondered aloud whether a strong president would be more effective than the parliamentary model of government.

Indira Gandhi was still very new as Prime Minister. 'After Nehru, what?' (or rather, 'who?') was the big question. *Indian Politics after Nehru* was the title of a book published to guide people preparing to vote in the 1967 elections. (The Jan Sangh was one of the new parties identified in the survey: the predecessor of the BJP). India was sailing into uncharted waters. Nehru had been a sick man in his last years. He never recovered from the 1962 Chinese invasion. In my first term at university back in England, we had gone round the shops that November, collecting money for Indian soldiers. Nehru's successor, Lal Bahadur Shastri, did not live long enough to leave any impact. 'Shastri – damn fool!' was Shetty's rather unkind verdict as we travelled together on the train. He didn't explain why and I was too shy to ask.

In the 1967 elections, the Congress monopoly began to be shaken. It retained power at the centre, but in the south the Dravida Munnetra Kazhagam became the first regional party, while Kerala and West Bengal elected 'United Front' governments, both led by a branch of the Communist Party (which had already divided more than once). The DMK promised radical change. It was strongly Dravidian: anti-Brahmin, anti-Sanskrit, seeking a renaissance of Dravidian history, language and culture. The United Front in Kerala did not last long, but in West Bengal it has continued, in different forms, for over thirty years.

The press was generally subservient to the government, which controlled the import of paper. There was no alternative to the government-run All India Radio, except Radio Ceylon with its very popular music programmes. Books like Ronald Segal's *The Crisis of India* were banned; V. S. Naipaul's *India: an Area of Darkness* was unofficially discouraged.

The previous twenty years had seen the development of the controlled economy, tightly regulated business and centralised planning, with great importance given to the Five-Year Plans and the all-powerful Planning Commission. Most people assumed that this was still the way forward, though in practice the government was more centre than left (perhaps more *chalta hai* – 'that's how it goes' – than strictly *laissez faire*). A few argued for a less regulated, more open market, with more openness to the West. But with the Cold War still raging everywhere, non-alignment was the preferred policy. Even after Nehru's death, Tito and Suharto, Nasser and Sadat, the pillars of the Non-Aligned Movement, were still household names, with Castro soon joining them. On the other hand, extremist movements on the left like the Naxalites of West Bengal and Andhra Pradesh were active and violent.

In 1969 Indira Gandhi struck. She split the Congress, removing the old guard who thought they could control her when they put her in power. She nationalised the major banks and abolished the 'privy purses' of the former rulers of the princely states, thus establishing her socialist and populist credentials. Abu Abraham of the *Indian Express*, with his gentle but biting humour, was my favourite cartoonist. One of his cartoons of the time was captioned *Ek Phool, Do Mali* ('One Flower, Two Gardeners') after a popular cinema love story. It showed the Congress Party, a struggling plant in its flowerpot, being diligently watered by Indira Gandhi on the one side (Congress I), and the old guard on the other (Congress S).

Consumer goods were still very restricted. Fridges were a luxury, air-conditioning even more so. Washing machines were virtually unknown. Who needed them with *dhobis* and domestic servants? Three models of car were available: the Ambassador, the Standard or the Fiat (now Premier). People waited years to buy a Vespa or Lambretta scooter, the only two models available. Or they could opt for an Enfield, Rajdoot or Jawa motorcycle. Nothing else. Another of Abu's cartoons showed Leonid Brezhnev, the Soviet leader, visiting India. Brezhnev's weakness for foreign cars was well known and he had been given a Cadillac on his recent visit to the USA. In the cartoon Indira Gandhi was presenting him with an Ambassador car drawn by two bullocks.

Many middle-class people looked abroad for their expectations of a better life. A passport (difficult to obtain) could literally be the passport to education or a job in the West. The friends I had made at university had returned to India with high ideals for a career in public service or business. Most of them are still in India, thirty-five years later. But at that time many others were looking for ways to leave, at least for a time.

Mahatma Gandhi was still a figure of immense admiration and respect. Living Gandhians like Vinoba Bhave, Jaiprakash Narayan and Khan Abdul Gaffar Khan ('The Frontier Gandhi') were greatly respected. Freedom fighters

were honoured and a jail sentence under the British was still
the main qualification for a seat in the Lok Sabha. But
Gandhiji seemed to be remembered more in sorrow than with
conviction. So few appeared to be able to follow his ideals,
whether in political life, personal discipline or communal
harmony.

In the late 1960s the right direction for India seemed
shrouded in uncertainty. There were certainly more questions
than answers. There was still plenty of idealism, along with
the usual mixture of cynicism. To describe a person as a
'social worker' (usually wearing *khadi* – homespun) was an
honourable title. But for most people it was the daily struggle
to keep going, without too much conviction or enthusiasm
about the future.

2
Kerala: The Beginnings of Christianity in India

One gets the impression that a St Thomas Christian is born and not made.

— *Benedict Vadakkekara*

The Indian Christian (in Southern India at least) has not succeeded in shaking off his heredity of centuries ... he is a staunch observer of castes.

— *Anantakrishna Ayyar*

One of the more dramatic effects of conversion emerges through an analysis of the position of women.

— *Geoffrey Oddie*

The first few weeks in Madras were very busy as I tried to catch up with my new situation and learn my job. Around a hundred students from various states, mostly from the south and northeast, were studying at the college.

Dr Gupta was passionate about the message that had changed his life. He had been brought up to believe that God comes into the world, in one of his incarnations, to uphold the good and punish the sinners. But then he had heard those preachers who said that Jesus came into the world to *save*

sinners, not to punish them. That had aroused his curiosity.
He obtained a Bible. Being careful with money (at least with
his own money), he managed to borrow one, rather than
buying it. He devoured its contents and was captivated by
the figure of Jesus and his offer of peace and forgiveness.
He was liberated from his guilt and felt he could overcome
his temptations. At considerable personal cost he followed
his convictions and wanted others to know what he had
discovered. His family cut him off and he started out on the
journey that eventually led him to the college in Madras.
There he passed on his passion and convictions to the
students.

I shared those convictions. But I was facing questions.

How did this message of forgiveness and relationship
with God relate to the social and economic problems that
were both immediate and obvious? I walked down a street
near Broadway, in the business quarter, past people living on
the pavement. The south-east monsoon had just started and
they were wet and miserable. I felt sick and helpless when I
saw them. Behind our college were rows and rows of
thatched huts. Not all the people living there were poor, but
many were. In the monsoon they also faced the misery of
flooding. Apart from this obvious poverty, I was beginning
to learn about other issues – endemic corruption, delays in
justice, lack of health care. I had left behind plenty of
problems in Britain. But here they just seemed to be so vast.
Where did one begin? What did I have to say about them?

A few months later I walked down the same street near
Broadway. Now the sun was shining and a woman was
cooking food on the pavement, while her children played
beside her. I saw they had dignity and hope, in the midst of
poverty. But I still wanted to know how the message I
believed in could help in any way to change their situation.

Another thing puzzled me, as I encountered Christianity in India.

On one hand, everything seemed different: the enthusiasm and simplicity of many whom I met, especially in the villages. The language was different, of course, and so was some of the music. I wasn't used to being woken at 4.30 a.m. by open-air preachers with loudspeakers. I was struck by the generous hospitality of the poorest people. I was surprised to see children crawling around in a church service, but I quite enjoyed the informality. I found a much stricter regulation of the relations between the sexes, with men and women generally sitting separately.

Yet I also found much that was familiar. Many of the songs were the same, whether old tunes played on the organ or new ones strummed on guitars. When I sat in St George's Cathedral with its neo-classical architecture, I could have been back in my college chapel (except for the fans turning above me). Many church buildings had European architecture, rows of pews inside, hymnbooks and prayer books that were either in English or translated from it. I passed the 'Scots Kirk' with its graceful steeple, or 'St Mary's Church' in 'Fort St George', where Robert Clive had been married. In one way it made it very easy: but I wondered if it should be like that. Was this part of the Christian message, or was it part of European culture? Was it just another appendix to the colonial enterprise?

Of course, there were exceptions. There were some churches where people sat on the floor, sang songs to quite different words and music, and joined together for a meal after worship.

I also became aware that people defined themselves by their community. There was a distinct Christian 'community'. If I asked somebody, 'Are you a Christian?' their answer

might be 'My name is John [or Thomas or Mary]. Of course
I am a Christian.' Or they might say, 'I was born to Christian
parents. Of course I am a Christian.' For them, being a
Christian seemed to mean being part of the Christian
community. It was a matter of birth and family, not
necessarily of personal conviction or spiritual experience.

Many years later, when I was travelling by train from
Delhi, one of my companions was convinced that everybody
in the West was a Christian. I tried to explain that this was
not the case; being a Christian was a matter of personal
belief, rather than your culture or community. I gave the
example of the Soviet Union, then still in existence, where
most people, at that time, were atheist despite the Christian
background of Russia. He agreed and it appeared that I had
made my point. But shortly afterwards we were talking about
a group of Christians in a village in Maharashtra. When I
told him about their struggle to learn to read the Bible in
Marathi, because of their low level of education, he looked
puzzled. 'But surely they understand English? They are
Christians, aren't they?'

What kind of Christianity was this? How did it start in
India? I needed to find out more.

I soon discovered that Kerala has a special place in the
history of Christianity in India. A sizeable section of our
students came from there, and after a few months I had the
opportunity of making a visit.

Kerala is different from any other part of India. You
usually travel there, as I did on that first journey from
Madras, by train overnight through the Western Ghats. I woke
up in a green world, away from the brown fields of the
previous day, with their scrubby thorn trees and the
occasional bright green rice paddy. In Kerala everywhere is
green, green, green – coconut palms, rubber, tapioca growing

out of the red earth, interwoven with green waterways. Your diet is rice, tapioca, coconut, fish, *uthapam* and twenty varieties of banana. You experience warm hospitality, inquisitive stares, and the most ferocious scrambles in India when the bus arrives.

Shoko: A New Beginning

In between visiting Kerala, trying to teach, learning the culture and failing to learn Tamil, I was corresponding with Shoko, the Japanese girl I had met on MV Laos. She had been brought up in a Buddhist family. As a teenager she heard about Jesus and committed herself to follow him. She came to visit India in 1968. We got engaged and six months later we were married, in Madras. It was exciting to begin our new home together, in many ways another 'conversion' experience, as we entered our cross-cultural marriage.

Soon afterwards we were invited to Kerala for a conference. It was my third visit.

Our hosts took us to a beautiful beach, with white sand gleaming against the blue sea and sky. 'This is where the Apostle Thomas landed,' they told us. A mile inland they showed us a lake where he did his first miracle.

Thomas

Thomas was one of the twelve disciples of Jesus, the inner circle. After Jesus' death and resurrection they scattered in different directions to preach his revolutionary message of love and forgiveness. Peter and Paul, the best known, travelled west through the Mediterranean world, and eventually to Rome. Thomas travelled east, following the trade routes to India, especially the spice route. One early document refers to his going to North India; others refer to the South.

Historians tell us that it can't be *proved* that Thomas actually came. Indians *know* that Thomas did come. Certainly there was constant traffic between South India and the Mediterranean at that time. Plenty of Roman coins from the period have been found in Kerala. If he came on the southern route he would have had a twenty-day journey by sailing ship, longer than our journey from Marseilles to Bombay. The ships carried horses and other cargo on the way out and spices on the return. Thomas would probably have slept in the hold with the horses, in smelly conditions. He is believed to have preached on the western Malabar coast and then travelled to the Coromandel coast on the east, where he preached and was killed. San Thome Cathedral in Chennai marks the place of his preaching; St Thomas Mount, on the way to the airport, the place of his death.

On the Malabar side, a number of families adopted the new faith. After some initial resistance they seem to have been accepted by local society and remained as a self-contained group for centuries. They had connections with the church of Antioch, in Syria, and so became known as Syrian Christians. Today the churches in Kerala are distributed in three major divisions: the old Orthodox Syrian tradition (now divided into several groups), the Roman Catholics and a range of independent Protestant groups.

The teaching of Christ may have gone to other parts of India in those early centuries. Apart from the northern tradition already mentioned, there are fascinating parallels and connections with devotional movements in Hinduism and with writings like the *Bhagavad Gita*, or the *Thirukkural*, the Tamil book of wisdom by Thiruvalluvar.

Any visitor to Kerala is struck by the depth and strength of tradition in the Christian community – twenty centuries of it, going back long before Christianity reached most of

Europe. As the congregation comes out of church on a Sunday morning, the men stand around with their white *dhotis* and black umbrellas, looking dignified and serious. Some of the older women still wear the traditional blouse, upper cloth and white *dhoti*, tucked up into a fan shape at the back. Back in the 1960s young men travelling from their jobs in Madras or Bombay would board the train wearing their 'city' clothes – drainpipe trousers, shirt (perhaps coloured) and shoes (no jeans or Nike trainers in those days). By next morning they would have changed into *dhoti*, white shirt and sandals, ready to go home. Those who had grown moustaches would shave them off, knowing their elders frowned on them.

But along with this conservative appearance, we found that Kerala's Christians were part of vibrant social movements in the state. Kerala has one of the highest literacy rates in India and is one of the only states where communists have been voted in and out of government, once on their own, more often as part of a 'United Front' coalition. Despite the relative lack of industry, there is a high level of prosperity, with a good measure of equal distribution (though some groups are still marginalised). Infant and maternal mortality rates are as low as anywhere in the world.

Some Christians in Kerala have had a close relationship with Marxism. They have seen the mission of the church as essentially horizontal, concerned with people's lives here and now, rather than in the hereafter. Salvation means 'liberation' or 'humanisation'. The church must be in 'solidarity with the struggles of the oppressed'. Back in the 1960s the Student Christian Movement expressed this emphasis through its conferences and literature. One of the best-known leaders, M. M. Thomas, began his career as a student activist with a decidedly Marxist viewpoint. He went on to become a distinguished writer and international Christian statesman, focussing on the relation between religion and society. One of the few Christians to oppose Indira Gandhi's Emergency, he ended his career as Governor of Nagaland under the V. P. Singh government in the 1990s.

Reflection : First Impressions

We were beginning to get an idea, though of course it was still very superficial, of the profile of Christianity in South India. Christianity had clearly taken deep root in Kerala. It had contributed significantly to social change, and many Kerala Christians were totally committed to continuing that tradition. In fact they had joined forces with others, whether Congress or Communist, as social activists. Here was an approach that did not seem to emphasise conversion as much as social action.

But that raised questions. Was Christianity just one community among the others? In Kerala there had been conversions at the very beginning. But now the Christians seemed to have been encapsulated within the community mosaic – in quite a favourable position. The 'secular correctness' of the time said that it should continue like that. But was the message of Christ only for the Christian community? In that case it was not universal. Or was it only a message of social ideals, to be made use of by people of all shades of religious and political opinion? In that case, where was its distinctiveness?

There was still a lot more to learn. We had seen how Christianity began in India. But how had it spread?

3

Coromandel: The Spread of Christianity in India

Conversion is a subversion of secular power.
— *Gauri Viswanathan*

The singular objective of all churchmen in India is conversion, or to use their term, the harvesting of souls for Jesus.
— *Arun Shourie*

Christianity... did not systematically convert, but its presence acted as an irritant to existing religious belief and provoked self-questioning, reformist reactions.
— *Sunil Khilnani*

I woke early, with a splitting headache and sore throat. I had spent the night on the floor of a photographer's studio in Nagercoil, along with Ananda Rao, a colleague at the Bible Institute, and two students. We were on our way to Kanya Kumari, to see India's southernmost point.

We stepped out into the street. It was still dark. Sleepy-looking men brushed past us, as we went into the nearest cafe. Behind the cashier were the familiar pictures – gods and goddesses, Gandhiji and Nehru – joined by two less

expected: John F. Kennedy and Jesus Christ. We walked
down to the sea, in time to see the sun rise over the Bay of
Bengal, while we could also dip our feet in the Indian Ocean
and the Arabian Sea. We watched the waves breaking over
Vivekananda Rock, where they were beginning to build an
enormous temple. We admired the devotion of the pilgrims
and avoided the attentions of the souvenir sellers. Then we
moved a few hundred metres down to the beach where the
fishermen were just landing their boats.

The fishermen were dark-skinned and deep-chested, wiry
and strong. Their boats were made of four thick lengths of
wood, lashed together. In these, with barely enough room for
them to stand, they braved the waves, sailing their boats out
at night and returning in the morning with their catch. The
fish spilled out on the beach and were collected by the
women into baskets. Today's catch was moderate. They could
make a fortune overnight, with a good catch. But they could
also lose it overnight, as they loved gambling.

Further up the beach were the huts in which they lived.
Small children stared at us, as we took off our trousers. The
fishermen had offered to take us out for a few minutes in
one of their boats. It was relatively calm and the sun was
sparkling on the water. We came back exhilarated but soaked.
The fishermen's life was clearly adventurous, hard and risky.
They were tough but superstitious. 'They won't call each
other by name while in the boats,' our guide told us. 'They
think it's unlucky.'

The fishermen were Christian. The Roman Catholic
missionary, Francis Xavier, who is buried in Goa, had come
down to the Coromandel coast in 1542, and thousands of
fishermen, a whole people group, had become Christians.
Xavier taught them the Ten Commandments, the Lord's
Prayer and a basic creed. They had retained their Christian

identity, but perhaps not much more. Their lifestyle appeared to have changed very little over the centuries.

Other Catholic missions followed, in different parts of Tamil Nadu. The first Protestant missionaries came to Tranquebar, further up the Coromandel coast, in 1705. They were Germans, sent by the King of Denmark, with the support of an English missionary society. They were followed by others over the next hundred years.

Ziegenbalg, the first Protestant missionary, was a hard worker. Within a year, he had begun preaching in Tamil, and soon began work on translating the Bïble and encouraging literacy. (When I read about him, I was impressed and envious: I never got beyond a basic level of street Tamil). As people heard his preaching and some became Christians, he provided education and found himself increasingly drawn into the social needs of the new converts. For example, he discovered that there was no provision for girls to be educated, except the *devadasis*, who learned music and dance. So Ziegenbalg started the first school for girls.

One major effect of the missionaries' work on the Coromandel coast was a renaissance of the Tamil language. When the DMK swept to power in Tamil Nadu in 1967 they erected huge statues, along the Marina Beach in Chennai, of the heroes and heroines of Tamil culture. Three of them are missionaries – Beschi, Caldwell and Pope – who produced grammars and dictionaries, and translated Tamil classics.

Not everything was plain sailing. The missionaries came up against different social and religious structures. Some responded aggressively, others tried to accommodate to them.

Francis Xavier seems to have taken a strong line. He wrote

When I have finished baptising the people, I order them

to destroy the huts in which they keep their idols; and I have them break the statues of their idols into tiny pieces, since they are now Christians. I could never come to an end of describing to you the great consolation which fills my soul when I see idols being destroyed by the hands of those who had been idolaters. (*The Letters and Instructions of Francis Xavier*, Gujarati Sahitya Prakash, 1993: quoted in Chowgule 1999*, p. 24)

Along with the destruction of idols might go change of name, clothes, diet, music, art and other aspects of the local culture.

Others took a different approach, viewing the local culture much more positively. Ziegenbalg, for example, generally tried to keep within South Indian culture, particularly in his schools. He had a high regard for Hindu ethical standards, as compared to European.

But in general, conversion was seen by many as a threat to family, community and culture.

Why?

I thought about the fishermen on the beach, responding to Xavier. What did they feel about the changes they experienced? How deep had they gone? I thought about Ziegenbalg and the early Christians further north in Tamil Nadu. I thought about the Christians I knew in Madras. Some had been Christians for centuries, like the Syrian Christians. Others were second or third generation. Some had been converted themselves, like Dr Gupta. What had been going on in their lives? What had made them change? How had they become different from their Hindu or Muslim countrymen? What was the relation between conversion and culture?

---

*   Books referenced only by author's name and year of publication are listed with full details in 'For Further Reading', pp. 153-54

Conversion and Change

Recently Gauri Viswanathan has thrown light on the questions I was struggling to formulate all those years ago. Her book *Outside the Fold: Conversion, Modernity, and Belief* (Princeton University Press, 1998) is a study of religious conversions in the context of India *and* Britain from around 1800 to 1956, the year when Dr B. R. Ambedkar, the noted political leader, was converted to Buddhism.

She argues that conversion was a response to change and to the 'realignment between state, religion, culture and empire' in *both* Britain and India. In *both* places conversion was a disturbing affirmation of the right to freedom of belief and practice.

In Britain, those who broke away from the prevailing Church of England were affirming the possibility that people of different religious conviction could be part of the same nation, as equal citizens. This was not the case in the eighteenth century: they were excluded from the universities, from parliament, even from voting rights. It took over a century, from around 1780 to 1880, for the necessary legal changes to be made. The repeal of the Test and Corporation Acts was the first legal milestone that began to lift restrictions from Protestant 'dissenters' in 1828 and Catholics in 1829. Jews and atheists had to wait much longer.

These changes were threatening to many, because 'conversion unsettles the boundaries by which selfhood, citizenship, nationhood and community are defined, exposing them as permeable borders' (Viswanathan, 1998, p. 16).

In India around the same time, some converts to Christianity faced opposition from family and community. In some cases they were excommunicated and considered dead (by a legal fiction of 'civil death'). As a result they lost the right to their property and inheritance. Some went to court, and in 1850 the Caste Disabilities Removal Act was passed. This defended their right to their ancestral inheritance, but only at the cost of *not* recognising their new religious and spiritual identity. They could claim their ancestral property only because the law considered them to be still part of their former religious structure. Their position was similar to that of married women in Britain, who lost all their rights to property on marriage, until the Married Women's Property Act became law in 1870.

Both Hindu and Muslim society *and* the colonial power regarded conversion as something disruptive, though perhaps for different reasons.

The majority religious communities from which the converts had come might view their change of belief as divisive and upsetting to their customs and community life. In some cases they might feel it a threat to their position as a community, especially if significant numbers were involved. Where this happens, Gauri Viswanathan comments,

> Dominant communities prefer to use the term 'proselytism' rather than 'conversion' to indicate the forcible nature of religious change. The term also carries with it a baggage of associations that identify religious change as an effect of manipulation, propagandistic activity, loss of individual self-control and will power, and sustained political mobilization. The use of the term 'proselytism' further denies subjectivity, agency, or choice to the subject and replaces individuals with masses as the unit of analysis. (Viswanathan, 1998, p. 87)

The British colonial power, on the other hand, found that religious conversions upset the categories into which they had divided the majority communities – primarily Hindu and Muslim – which they wished to leave undisturbed as far as possible. While they developed a uniform criminal code, they maintained separate personal laws for these two communities, covering areas such as marriage, divorce, adoption and inheritance. As a result, when dealing with converts on these matters, they found it awkward, if not impossible, to take into account the converts' inner, personal and spiritual experience. They dealt with them only on the basis of the legal community to which they were supposed to belong. The Indian Succession Act of 1865 created personal laws for Indian Christians. This gave them legal rights but it also meant that being a 'Christian' was defined as being part of a different legal community, rather than as having made a spiritual and religious choice.

So the division between communities hardened. It became impossible to continue as part of both. You had to choose. The change of legal status was often followed by other changes – name, diet and clothes. So conversion was seen very much in these external changes, rather than as a personal and spiritual experience.

The legacy of those decisions is still with us today. How do we hold together the inner, spiritual meaning of conversion with its outer social and cultural implications?

Conversion and Colonialism

The other big question raised in all discussions of the early missionaries' work is their relation to colonialism. It is often assumed that the missionaries worked hand in glove with the colonial power: two sides of the same coin. The reality is more complex. Brijraj Singh has looked carefully at the issues in his recent study: *Ziegenbalg; The First Protestant Missionary to India* (Oxford University Press, 1999).

Apart from the Portuguese, no Christian missionaries in India were directly linked to the colonial powers. In fact the East India Company did not allow any missionaries in the territory it controlled until 1813. The early missionaries seem to have had an ambivalent relationship with the growing colonial and economic activities of the European powers. On one hand, they were sometimes supported by them and identified with them. In general they were not opposed to the colonial enterprise. But on the other hand, their aims were different, and their close contact with Indians brought changes in their attitudes as they learned more about the culture and language. Sometimes the missionaries came into conflict with the colonial values and openly opposed them, protesting on behalf of poorer or oppressed groups against injustice.

William Carey, working in Calcutta in the early nineteenth century, joined forces with Hindu social reformers to press for social change, resulting in the abolition of *sati* and other reforms. Fifty years later, missionaries in Bengal stood out against the indigo planters (both British and Indian) who were exploiting their workers. At great personal cost they organised the workers and successfully withstood the pressure of the planters – James Long, a missionary, was accused of libel and imprisoned. Others campaigned against alcoholism, child marriage and other social evils that they saw. In some places whole communities experienced uplift and change. On most of these issues they worked alongside Hindu social reformers. While part of their concern was to facilitate and strengthen their preaching work, their major motivation was humanitarian. They were moved by anger at injustice and exploitation and wanted to help those who needed protection.

So were they colonialists? Brijraj Singh concludes that Ziegenbalg, at least, 'though not without colonial leanings, [was] not a colonialist' (Singh, 1999, p. 163).

Reflection

I was still trying to learn. Our visit to the fishermen had raised a lot of questions. I didn't doubt the sincerity and hard work of the early missionaries. But I was becoming aware of social and cultural issues from the past that were still relevant. I wanted to meet people who were working with sensitivity to these issues.

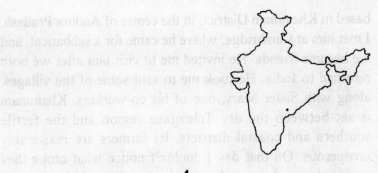

4

Unravelling Caste:
Walking Through Villages in
Andhra Pradesh

> Hinduism does not mind conversion, so long as the
> convert continues to perform the task enjoined on him by
> his caste affiliation.
>
> — *Gauri Viswanathan*
>
> In the 1930s the battle over untouchability was a matter
> of ritual purity and pollution. Today the violence between
> the different caste groups is based on their struggle for
> economic and political power, especially in situations
> where resources are scarce.
>
> — *André Béteille*

The bus stopped by the side of the country road and we
got down. There was no sign of life in any direction. 'This
is the way to the village,' said Azariah, pointing to a dusty
track running across the fields. The bus moved off and we
started walking, headed for a village two or three kilometres
away.

Korabundi Azariah is an evangelist, a travelling preacher

based in Khammam District, in the centre of Andhra Pradesh. I met him at Cambridge, where he came for a sabbatical, and we became friends. He invited me to visit him after we both returned to India. He took me to visit some of the villages, along with Sister Mary, one of his co-workers. Khammam is set between the dry Telengana region and the fertile southern and coastal districts. Its farmers are reasonably prosperous. On that day I couldn't notice what crops they were growing. I was only conscious of the path that seemed to wind on endlessly. Even in mid-December the afternoon sun of Andhra Pradesh was hot and the path was very dusty.

Suddenly we came round a bend and there was the village, on the other side of a stream. As we got closer, I could see a collection of rather miserable thatched huts to our right, on this side of the stream. 'That is the village *cheri* [slum],' said Azariah. 'There are some Christians living there, but I will not be able to go and visit them.'

I looked puzzled.

'If I go there, I may not be welcome in the homes of the village farmers. You see, these people come from what is called the Scheduled Castes. They used to be Untouchables. Sister Mary will go and visit them. The Christians understand why I don't go there.'

I looked more puzzled. I was face to face for the first time with the complexities of caste.

Caste

Everybody in India knows what it is, and everybody explains it differently.

One reason, of course, is that it really is complex. How did the caste system begin? How long ago? Did it really start from the *varna* system, which would suggest that it was based on skin colour – or was that a later rationalisation?

Did the Aryans really invade from the north-west and use caste to maintain the distinction between themselves and the darker-skinned local people? Or were they there from the beginning as well...? The Vedas tell the story of four castes coming out of the body of Vishnu – the Brahmins from his head, the Kshatriyas from his body, the Vaisyas from his thighs, the Sudras from his feet. How significant is that? Was it meant to show the inter-dependence of the different groups, living together in a village community like the one we were visiting? Or did it result in reinforcing the sacred power of the Brahmins?

The other key word for caste is *jati* – occupational groups based on hereditary professions. There are hundreds of them. How do they fit in? If that was the origin of caste, how did it get combined with the *varna* system? How do the different *jatis* correspond to the four main divisions of *varnashrama dharma*? Is caste religious or social in origin – or both? Can you change your *jati*, or can you move it to another division of the *varna* system? The questions go on and on.

The other reason that people explain caste differently is that their perspectives and experiences are different. If you belong to one of the 'forward' castes you may see it as a beneficial way of absorbing different social groups, enabling them to live together in harmony and inter-dependence. In the old village society, the landowners would look after their workers. The craftsmen would serve the rich and receive trade and patronage in return. The priests would ensure the prosperity and well-being of all through carrying out the proper sacrifices and rituals. And so on. Everybody in their proper place. It was like the Victorian hymn: 'The rich man in his castle, the poor man at his gate.'

That was the ideal.

The makers of India's constitution recognised the

inequalities that actually existed. They abolished untouchability and introduced positive discrimination to help the outcastes and backward castes to break through the barriers. Their success in doing so – which has been enormous – has resulted in greater equality, but in some places greater tension, violence and caste wars, especially in feudal states like Bihar. André Béteille, a prominent Indian sociologist, comments:

> In the 1930s the battle over untouchability was a matter of ritual purity and pollution. Today the violence between the different caste groups is based on their struggle for economic and political power, especially in situations where resources are scarce.

Caste is still the major fixed structure of Hinduism, providing stability, security and inter-dependence, as well as being an instrument of oppression and inequality. Trying to take a balanced view of caste seems to be like trying to ride two horses at once. The result is inevitable. Gandhiji agonised over caste, campaigning for the outcastes and criticising the upper castes. 'Caste has nothing to do with religion,' he said. 'It is harmful both to spiritual and national growth.' But he still regarded caste as the essence of Hinduism:

> *Varnashrama* does attach to birth. A man cannot change his *Varna* by choice ... I believe that if Hindu society has been able to stand it is because it is founded on the caste system.

All religions in India have struggled with caste. There have been many movements of protest or reform, wanting to abolish caste distinctions. Buddha, Kabir, Guru Nanak, the *bhakti* movements – all spoke out and acted against the divisiveness of caste and the dominance of the upper castes. Yet many Muslims, Sikhs or Christians, who in theory oppose caste, acknowledge caste distinctions in one way or another. Even the Neo-Buddhists, who followed their leader Dr Ambedkar into Buddhism to escape their status at the bottom of the pile, do not appear to have benefited a great deal. I have travelled with them a couple of times when hundreds of them have taken over the trains going into Mumbai for the celebration of Dr Ambedkar's birthday. Thirty-three were crammed into our little section of the compartment, intended for eight. We literally had to climb over them to get out at our stop. Most were in a very jolly mood, though some who couldn't get on board smashed windows or even tried to overturn the train. They saw themselves as pilgrims – entitled to free travel in any part of the train.

Early Christian missionaries were at a loss as they confronted the caste system. Robert de Nobili, a Catholic scholar in Madurai in the seventeenth century, felt he should identify with the Brahmins as a scholar and religious leader. Later German Lutherans compared caste to the hierarchical class system of eighteenth-century Europe, so did not' intervene. Others were more egalitarian and insisted that distinctions between higher and lower castes should be abolished, as incompatible with the Christian gospel. They saw the oppression of the backward and scheduled castes and wanted to be on the side of the poor.

The test came when people attended the Holy Communion: did they sit together or separately? Did they drink from the same cup?

Some missionaries insisted that new believers must 'break caste' as a sign of their equality in Christ. Some high-caste people welcomed this, as a revelation of equality and dignity. For Lakshmibai Tilak in 1900, who had spent her whole life preserving her Chitpavan Brahmin purity,

> It happened in the twinkling of an eye ... All the chains
> of caste distinction, that had bound my mind so tightly,
> burst and fell rattling down ... Did God create different
> castes of man? ... then why did the same God not also
> arrange an order of castes in the animal world? ... enough,
> my caste distinctions were gone. From that day on I would
> hold all equal. The very roots of my caste pride were gone.
> (Tilak, 1900, p. 192)

Some Christians extended this, emphasising certain
outward aspects of their new cultural identity which had very
little to do with the gospel. Dr Subbamma, now a church
leader in Andhra Pradesh, described the feast on the occasion
of her baptism. 'Tonight you are going to eat beef,' she was
told, joyfully and triumphantly, by the local Christians.
Coming from a Hindu background, Subbamma felt revolted.
But she told herself: 'I have given up so much for Christ.
This will only be a small sacrifice.' She choked down the
beef. But later she wondered why she had needed to go
through such a 'cultural circumcision'. In fact, many Indians
who follow Christ are vegetarian.

The arguments continue in the church today, where caste
distinctions are still alive and well. Liberation theologians –
influenced as much by Marxism as by the gospel – argue that
the church's mission is to join the struggle of the poor and
oppressed of all faiths. Others oppose caste distinctions
within the church. In Chennai, a recent Bishop of the Church
of South India spent much of his time and energy replacing
higher-caste leaders with Dalits. Others argue that caste is
part of Indian society and can't be just wished away. The
church must accommodate it in some way, at least in the early
stages. The debate continues.

At the end of the nineteenth century and the beginning
of the twentieth, large numbers of people belonging to the

scheduled caste groups decided to become Christians. In North India thousands of Chamars (originally leather workers, and so outside the caste system) became Christians, following the step originally taken by a man called Ditt. He was not particularly a leader but his action had an impact on his extended family and from there it spread to others within the community. In South India there were large movements, especially in Andhra Pradesh. Apart from Kerala and the North East, the vast majority of Christians in India come from this Scheduled Caste background. Of course, there are Christians from many other caste backgrounds as well.

In the 1930s the issue of conversion became political, as the British announced their intention of separate electorates for the different religious communities. They proposed a separate electorate for the untouchables, which was welcomed by their leader, Ambedkar. A 'schedule' of the relevant castes was prepared (hence the name 'Scheduled Castes'). Gandhi's Poona Pact with Ambedkar changed the equation by ensuring that the untouchables remained within the Hindu electorate, though with separate reserved seats. Despite this, Hindu leaders have always felt uneasy at the thought of conversion by members of the scheduled castes, whether to Buddhism, Islam or Christianity.

Untouchability is acknowledged by many Hindus as a blot on the record of Hinduism. Dr Karan Singh has described their 'ill-treatment over the centuries' as 'a standing disgrace to the otherwise remarkable achievements of Hindu civilisation'.

In 1950 a Presidential Order defined which of the Scheduled Castes were eligible for the benefits and positive discrimination promised by the constitution. It ruled that only Hindus or Sikhs could be Scheduled Caste and that the

benefits should not apply to those from other religions like
Muslims and Christians, even if they came from a Scheduled
Caste background. It argued that Islam and Christianity did
not recognise caste distinctions. Later judgements extended
the benefits to Jains and Buddhists from a Scheduled Caste
background. Some Christians have campaigned for these
benefits to be given to Christians from Scheduled Caste
backgrounds, since they may be as much economically and
socially deprived as those who are still Hindu.

The Village Farmers

All this was completely unknown to me at that time, as
I stood with Azariah outside the village. Sister Mary turned
to the right to visit the Christians living in the untouchable
section. Azariah and I crossed the stream and entered the
village.

The farmers lived in well-constructed houses, with
thatched or tiled roofs. Each stood in its own enclosed space
with room for their buffaloes and for growing vegetables. The
farmer's wife welcomed us. It was bliss to pour water on our
dusty feet and sit down on the verandah. It wasn't quite so
blissful, later in the afternoon, to try to bathe before the
evening meal. The bathroom was a small space in the corner
of the garden, enclosed with palm thatch screens. You took
a brass pot of water and balanced precariously on the large
flat stone in the middle, trying to avoid slipping off and
getting dust and mud on your feet and legs. The toilet? The
fields were not too far away ...

That evening the farmer's wife served us food before she
served the rest of the family. We ate separately, off banana
leaves, which could be disposed of. Then we sat to talk with
the farmer and his family, now all back from their work.

Azariah introduced me. *'Telugu raadu* [he doesn't

understand Telugu].' Despite this, he usually asked me to say something in each of the houses we visited. Near Christmas it was appropriate to tell the story of Jesus' birth and something of its meaning. Azariah would continue, telling them about Jesus and inviting them to consider him. He had visited many of these homes over the preceding years and quite a number had expressed their desire to follow Jesus for themselves. Azariah encouraged them to stay within their cultural and social setting and pray to Jesus within their families. He would then invite them to come, two or three times a year, to a central place where they would meet other people from the neighbouring villages who were also interested to follow Jesus. This gave them an opportunity for more concentrated teaching and interaction with each other. By the time I met him, several hundred of these village farmers had become followers of Jesus. They had received baptism but not yet formed any 'church' or built any church buildings. Azariah wanted them to stay within their cultural setting.

His approach was gentle, persuasive and respectful. The next day we visited several homes, including a busy, rather harassed housewife, who clearly had a tendency to grumble and be irritated. As we talked, Azariah looked up at the pictures of her gods on the wall. 'Sister, let me take those for you,' he said. 'Next time I go to the town I will change them for a beautiful picture of Jesus. That will help you to pray.' The woman seemed happy to accept the offer and we took the pictures with us.

Reflection

Culture and faith

Walking in the villages with Azariah introduced me to a new thought. I had just been made aware of some of the

issues raised by caste. It began to explain the sense of
separateness of the Christian church that I had encountered
so far, and some of the questions of culture and community.
But was it possible for people to follow Jesus without leaving
their community? Was this the way to deal with those
questions?

If so, how would followers of Jesus from various
communities express their faith? Would it look very different
from the church life I had seen? How would following Christ
bring change in other areas of life?

What about caste discrimination? I was still thinking of
those Christians in the Scheduled Caste section of the village,
whom we never met. Did they meet the farmers who had
begun to follow Jesus? Did they see a difference in them and
were they acknowledged as brothers?

Social action?

Was the new faith in Christ making any difference to the
social conditions in the villages? The farmers appeared quite
contented, and clearly they themselves were not poor. But
what about the obvious need for health and education in the
villages as a whole? What would be the best way to provide
for them, a way that would be just and fair without
perpetuating dependence? What about the exploitation that
often takes place in rural areas? Was there any change in that?

At that time when I met him, Azariah did not appear to
have any social programme. Far from 'enticing' people, there
was no systematic plan for dealing with social issues.

As we returned from our village tour, we met the local
Family Planning worker. Azariah greeted her. 'How are
things going?' he asked. Not too well, it seemed. She felt
frustrated because nobody took her very seriously. She was
underpaid by the government, and tempted to do little.

In 1967 nobody really knew what the answer was to the 'population problem'. It was assumed that the issue was simply one of conception and how to prevent it. The obvious weakness of that approach was that people had all kinds of reasons for wanting children. They might be seen as: a blessing from God; a source of labour; the hope of security in old age; a son's hand to light the funeral pyre ... You needed plenty, because who knew how many would survive beyond childbirth or infancy? 'May you be the mother of a hundred sons' summed up the ultimate blessing of a large family. Naturally people resisted contraception and especially sterilisation. If these other issues were not faced, the narrow focus on conception didn't work.

This was eight years before the Emergency, when Sanjay Gandhi's frustration with the slow progress of family planning led him to take extreme measures. Thousands were sterilised, with or without their consent. Some had never even had any children. Quotas were set for officials in every department. One railway official was reported to have stopped a train somewhere in Bihar and ordered all the men on board to have a vasectomy.

Azariah spoke kindly to the woman and encouraged her to keep going. But he didn't appear to have much to say on this burning social issue.

Walking in love

Walking with Azariah, I saw a man who 'walked in love'. He was a very caring person and his philosophy was 'to do the needful', as he put it, whatever that might be, and whoever the person was. His experience of God's love was his motivation. He took seriously the words of John, one of Jesus' disciples: 'If anyone sees his brother in need, yet closes his heart against his brother, how can he claim that he loves God? Our love should not be just words and talk; it must be true love, which shows itself in action. If this is how God loved us, then we should love one another.'

So for Azariah, words and actions went together. He met people's needs as he encountered them, without distinction. He was already supporting a number of children with their schooling and his home always had visitors who shared in the hospitality.

Azariah's approach was love, combined with the greatest respect for people's traditions and culture. To me it looked a very positive way forward. But was it too accommodating? Was there any challenge to injustice, or force for social change?

5
Working with the Community:
Rural Change in Maharashtra

Drink plenty of fluid; make a mixture of salt, sugar, nimbu
and water and drink it regularly. Don't let the person get
dried out, especially a baby.

— A nine-year-old girl.

When politicians come to the village, or police officials,
we don't bow down at their feet, as we used to. We know
they are just men, like us. We know we have dignity as
human beings.

— A villager

The road ran straight, with trees on either side. As we
got further away from the town the tarmac gave way more
frequently to mud and holes. We bumped on for several
miles, round bends and turns, across a dry stream-bed, past
open fields. Finally we reached a collection of low buildings:
The Comprehensive Rural Health Project (CRHP), in
Jamkhed, one of the poorer *taluks* in Ahmednagar District,
Maharashtra.

In 1971 Raj and Mabelle Arole, newly qualified doctors,
had arrived here to set up medical practice. Raj and Mabelle

both trained at the Christian Medical College and Hospital
in Vellore. He came from Maharashtra and she from Tamil
Nadu. They fell in love and got married. With their
qualifications they could have worked anywhere in India –
or abroad. But they had dedicated themselves to serve the
poor, so they returned to Maharashtra, where they looked for
an area which had been neglected. They settled on Jamkhed.

One of the things they had decided was that hospital
practice would not take up more than a third of their activity.
They wanted to work in the community. They began to visit
the villages to spend time with the people.

The village people found this strange: two doctors from
the city, who should be treated as *Barra Sahibs*, coming to
sit with them on their mud floors and discussing their needs.
But after the initial embarrassment, they began to realise that
these doctors were in earnest. They really did want to find
out what the village people were experiencing and what they
actually wanted.

Working with the Community

The work developed on principles that they partly
discovered themselves and partly gained from the experience
of others working on similar lines in different parts of the
world. It was a new approach in community health: you
sought to involve the community in taking responsibility for
their own health. It began from the felt needs of the
community, using local leaders and getting the community
to help actively. After a period of further study at John
Hopkins University in the USA, the Aroles began to develop
this new approach with great enthusiasm.

Not everybody appreciated this novel method, or the
impact that it was beginning to have. Not long after their
arrival, the Aroles found themselves surrounded at their clinic

by a hostile crowd. They were suspicious and threatening. 'You have come here to convert our people. Leave here at once or we will stone you.'

'No,' said the Aroles, 'we have not come here to convert you. We have come here to serve. We will not impose our beliefs on anybody, especially the poor.'

They were allowed to stay.

When we visited in 1983, there wasn't much, at first sight, to show for their efforts. The CRHP was a collection of small houses and huts. A low building contained the hospital wards, with the usual out-patients, operating theatre, labs, etc. The small staff went about their duties but the hospital didn't seem to be particularly busy.

Then we went to visit one of the villages.

Village Revolution

The village was unimpressive – a straggling collection of thatched huts, some built of mud, others of stone. The huts seemed dark and gloomy, with women crouched over stoves or making *chapatis* in the narrow passages. There was a kind of shed in the centre, a corrugated iron roof on wooden pillars with stones to hold it down. A group of villagers came there to meet the hospital staff who had brought us to visit them. After the introductions the villagers began to talk, in response to questions from the staff, about the changes they had experienced. A nine-year-old girl stood up and proceeded to tell us, with great confidence, what to do if you got fever.

'You take plenty of water, two tablets of paracetamol, keep the room well ventilated and sponge the person with a damp cloth to keep them cool.' No mention of calling the doctor.

What about diarrhoea – something very common to all?

'Drink plenty of fluid; make a mixture of salt, sugar, *nimbu* and water and drink it regularly. Don't let the person get dried out, especially a baby.' No mention of pills or doctors.

I was amazed. I knew that my colleagues in Pune, well-educated college teachers, did not know as much as this girl of nine. Like most other middle-class people, we would run to the doctor for the slightest thing. I remember how we went to the doctor when our first child, Sarah, was reluctant to drink milk. The doctor was a well-recommended paediatrician. She kept us waiting quite a while, and charged a hefty fee. When we finally saw her, she looked at the baby for a couple of minutes, then said, 'Put more sugar in the feed.'

This village girl knew how to deal with fever and diarrhoea, the two commonest illnesses – and she knew about Oral Re-hydration Therapy (ORT), the latest approach to dysentery and diarrhoea that had saved millions of children's lives around the world!

A man began to speak. 'In the old days, we couldn't walk through the village with our *chappals* on. We had to take them off and put them on our heads, to show respect to the high-caste people. Now we walk straight and hold up our heads, like anybody else. When politicians come to the village, or police officials, we don't bow down at their feet, as we used to. We know they are just men, like us. We know we have dignity as human beings.'

We listened with open mouths. I remembered Dr Ambedkar's characterisation of village life, with its inequality and exploitation, as the 'black hole' of Indian civilisation. What had brought such radical change in the highly stratified rural society?

People Taking Responsibility

Community health doesn't begin with a doctor treating

patients but with people taking responsibility for their own health. When the Aroles began work in a village, they would start by meeting village leaders. They would discuss what the village leaders saw as their immediate needs: a better water supply, perhaps, a new road, a school for the children. When the village leaders asked for their help, the Aroles would agree, on certain conditions:

'First, you will need to improve the access road, so that we can reach your village more easily. Then you must give us people to work with. Choose four or five women from the village, whom you recommend. We will train them to become village health workers.'

Once the conditions were agreed, the work would begin. The village health workers, often illiterate women, would be given training, along with a wooden box which was their medical chest. They would deal with all the basic sicknesses and attend the women at childbirth. Instead of bypassing the traditional village midwives, they would incorporate them: perhaps they would become village health workers themselves, and so would learn healthier practices. The hospital team would teach the villagers basic principles of hygiene. Fifty percent of common illnesses are caused by dirty water, inadequate drainage, mosquitoes or people going to the toilet in the wrong place, attracting flies or polluting the water supply. The villagers learned how to protect their water supply, to dig channels to take away the waste from the houses, and cover vessels to keep away flies and prevent mosquitoes.

Children's health was a top priority. One way to improve this was to organise a midday meal for all the village children. As they sat together to eat it, the health worker would go round checking their eyes for any sign of trachoma, the most common eye infection. They could carry out other basic health checks at the same time. The meal contained high-protein soya and other nutrients, which boosted the children's health. But it did more than that. While the CRHP provided the extra ingredients, every family was asked to contribute something to the meal. At first this was a handful of rice. When some of the poorer families found this difficult, they suggested salt. Even that was difficult for some, so finally it was agreed that everyone would bring a cup of water. The water was added to the pot where the food was cooking. Everybody was contributing to the community meal, for the benefit of their children.

But that raised questions for some people. A few parents began to think: if everybody was putting water into the common pot, that meant that water was coming from both the village wells - the well at one end of the village which the higher-caste people used, and the well outside the village which only the low-caste people used. Some higher-caste parents became upset and told their children they could no longer participate in the midday meal. But the children rebelled and told their parents they did not want to miss it. Reluctantly, the parents agreed. After a while they realised that the children were not suffering in any way. On the contrary, they were benefiting from the nutrition, the medical care and the community atmosphere. In a subtle way, caste barriers were being broken down and a broader community that included the whole village was being encouraged.

The health team targeted girls' education as well. In most village families, if anybody was educated at all, it was the boys. What was the point of educating the girls? Their role was to get married, bring up children and do the work in the home. The Aroles realised that if the girls were educated, especially in matters of health and hygiene, it would have a profound effect on the whole family and community. That's why the nine-year-old village girl knew more than most middle-class adults about looking after her family's health.

As the villagers took responsibility for their own health and hygiene, other needs and opportunities would arise. We saw a group of villagers planting trees on an empty hillside; another group was digging irrigation ditches and improving the layout of their fields. Both of these were community activities, in which a whole group of people needed to work together. The project proved to be the catalyst to enable them to do this. Back at the centre, in addition to the hospital, which saw only patients referred from the village health workers, there were other experiments going on. A wind vane powered a borewell bringing water for the project. A *gobar* gas tank produced cooking gas from cow dung. There were two large round huts with pointed thatched roofs that served as the conference centre. When villagers came to the project for training workshops or consultations, they did not have to enter concrete buildings like the government offices in the town. They did not have to sit on chairs, or squat on the floor while officials addressed them from their chairs. All could sit comfortably on the floor together. They could use the large huts for meeting, sleeping, eating or talking. They felt quite at home and in control of what was going on.

Change from the Inside

Profound changes were taking place, from the inside. New attitudes and values were being formed:
- Human beings have dignity and equality because they all come from the same source. All are made by the one God.
- We can take responsibility for our own health because we can understand some of the basic causes of illness.

- We can see the connection between health, education and living together as a community.
- We recognise the importance of doctors and other professionals. We can't treat everything ourselves, so we need them to teach and guide us.
- But we can stand on our own feet, alongside them.

I used to think that people needed medicine, or fertiliser, or bank loans, in order to improve their health, or agriculture or economy. Those are all needed, of course. **But real change begins in the mind and heart, from the inside.** When people's thinking changes, anything can happen. But without that, nothing lasting takes place.

Inner attitudes and values lead to change on the outside. Sometimes the village people would say, 'Today is not an auspicious day. We can't begin to plant our seeds, even though the weather seems just right and we are all ready to do it.'

The Aroles would reply, 'Every day is a day which God has made. So every day is good and none is inauspicious. You can begin planting today.'

The Aroles wanted to take away the mystique of the professional, the secret knowledge that gives them their power. That knowledge needs to be shared with all, without taking away the special function that the professional has. They opposed vested interests that kept ordinary people in subjection. Dr Arole thundered against the pharmaceutical companies who exploited people with their brand-name drugs at fancy prices. They were exploiting ordinary people and the medical profession was colluding with them, because it all helped to maintain their interests and profit.

What was the impact of the community health programme? In addition to what we saw, statistics gave their own story of the indicators of improved health and well being

– reduced infant and maternal mortality, higher literacy, reduced birth rate. The lower birth rate was not the result of a narrow emphasis on family planning. It was rather the result of better health and education. When people are secure in the basics of daily life, they are able to consider what family size is appropriate. The harassed family planning worker that I had seen in Andhra Pradesh could give way to more effective all-round health workers.

Wider Recognition

The CRHP at Jamkhed remained small. But it has obtained recognition across India and around the world, including the Magsaysay Award from the Philippines and the Padma Bhushan Medal awarded to Dr Arole. The Government of Maharashtra has used the centre for training its staff at both district and state levels. An internationally accredited Master's-level training programme shares the insights and experience learned with people from many countries.

Most important of all, the principles and skills are being used in large numbers of similar community health programmes across India. In Pune, where we lived for seven years, we met Dr Onawale, who was using the same principles in the urban slums behind the station. She had started the *Deep Griha* [Lighthouse] Society, working primarily with women. As Dr Onawale began with basic health needs, she found that one thing led to another. A major problem, she discovered, was alcoholism among the men, many of whom were unemployed. What little money the families had was being wasted. She needed to help the women to find ways of being self-supporting. She introduced tailoring classes. When women were enabled to buy a sewing machine and given basic skills, they could earn a significant amount. The next focus was the children's health, with teaching on nutrition and how to prevent or treat common illnesses. For older children, the need was a place to do their homework, away from the congestion and noise of their huts in the slum. The centre was opened for them to come and study in the evenings. Volunteers were found to teach reading and maths. Bill Goodman, a young graduate from England who had come to work with us, was one of those who gave some of his spare time to do this. It was a rewarding experience for him.

Reflection

At first sight community health programmes look untidy. People seem to be involved in a lot of different things, apparently unconnected and not always in the traditional 'health' areas. But they are all inter-connected, because that is what life is like.

Visiting the CRHP was a revelation to me. Here was a way to bring change in rural (and urban) communities. I saw it exemplified in the Aroles. It was not a matter of them 'bringing change'. The change came from the people, from the inside. The Aroles worked with them, following the connections and meeting needs as they arise. Working *with* the community, so that it can take responsibility for its own health and other needs, brings lasting results.

The Aroles did everything in the name and spirit of Jesus, whom they followed and who had inspired them to dedicate their lives to serving the poor. Their motivation was known to all. But they were concerned not to impose their views on anybody, or to create pressure, especially on the poor, who already faced such pressure in their daily lives. Perhaps they were also aware of the possible conflicts that might arise, and wanted to leave the situation open.

So what would be the form of the spiritual change that was taking place in the people of Jamkhed? Where would their newly discovered values lead them – to Marxism, Buddhism, Christian faith, a more humanised Hinduism? Or would they lead to caste wars, as had happened in Bihar? Or ...?

6
Taking Sides: Pioneer Work with Marginalised Children

You call me retarded,
you write about me as handicapped,
you speak about me as disabled,
but I just have some special needs.
— *A poster at Ashirvad*

What is needed is an intense, personal transformation and spiritual renewal,
as a result of which people are surprised by the way you live.
— *M. C. Mathew*

The Seventies were a decade of momentous political movements, though perhaps of little real change. Indira Gandhi put her stamp unmistakably on the decade. It really began in 1969 when she took over the Congress, out-manoeuvring her old opponents.

In 1971 Indira's position became even stronger when she assisted the leaders of East Pakistan in their revolt against West Pakistan. The Indian army went in to back the Mukti Bahini and Bangladesh was born. In order to protect herself,

Indira signed a twenty-year security treaty of friendship and mutual defence with the Soviet Union.

In the elections that followed she was returned to power with an overwhelming majority, which she used to implement her populist programmes. The constitution was amended to describe India as a 'Democratic' and 'Socialist' republic. *Garibi Hatao* (Away with poverty) was the slogan. Indira was unstoppable and there was no alternative.

But in 1974 another political force began to gather momentum. Jai Prakash Narayan, a former colleague of Nehru and a veteran freedom fighter, was working in Bihar mobilising peasants and especially students in a new organisation. His socialist credentials were even more impressive than Indira's. The Bihar movement was grassroots and growing rapidly. However, it had no electoral standing and could have been faced-down politically, given time. But time ran out when the Allahabad High Court ruled in June 1975 that Indira had been guilty of electoral malpractice and disqualified her from the Lok Sabha. Many observers assumed it was the end for her. They were wrong.

Indira's response was the Emergency. Salman Rushdie has dramatised the ruthless and sinister image of 'Indira of the Emergency' in his book *Midnight's Children*. Opposition leaders were put in jail, just like in the old days under the British. The press was totally muzzled and cowed (with one or two honourable exceptions). The Twenty-Point Programme took over. 'Talk less, work more' was the new slogan. Sanjay Gandhi emerged as the really ruthless one, implementing forced sterilisation programmes, demolishing Delhi slums and shifting thousands of the poor to new colonies one or two hours outside the city. People at first welcomed the discipline – the trains ran on time – but soon began to realise that their freedom was more precious.

In 1977 Indira surprised everybody again by announcing elections, indicating her basic instinct for democracy, but clearly expecting to win. The defection of Jagjivan Ram, a senior cabinet member, tipped the scales. The Janata Party came to power. Congress was out from the Centre for the first time in thirty years. Indira was out too, but not for long. The Janata Party, which had been stitched together in prison, fell apart in power. With Indira came Sanjay again, this time as a Member of Parliament, but still wielding enormous power and influence behind the scenes. The coded name for him was an 'ECP' – an 'extra-constitutional centre of power'. People loved him or hated him, but all feared him.

India's future might have been quite different but in 1980 Sanjay was killed in a flying accident and literally fell out of the sky. One of the most poignant images of the decade was Indira Gandhi after hearing the news – desolate, alone, a mother who had lost her son; a leader who had lost her political heir and her source of political strength.

The decade ended as it had begun, with Indira in control, with no other leaders in sight and no apparent alternative to the Nehru/Gandhi dynasty. Indira's deep concern for the poor and disadvantaged was undeniable. She really wanted social justice and was impatient with the forces of conservatism and vested interests, as she saw them – for example the courts, the middle class, the old guard among her political colleagues. She thought that nobody else could love India as she could, and that nobody else could serve India's people as she did. Her famous speech in Orissa, only the day before her assassination, summarised her passion:

'If I am killed, every drop of my blood will revitalise the country ...'

But at the end of the decade, it was unclear how much real social change had taken place.

One sign of the future was the newly inaugurated Maruti car plant outside Delhi. This joint collaboration with Suzuki of Japan was intended to produce the 'People's Car', a cheap and accessible alternative to the existing three models. Sanjay Gandhi was in charge but the project did not progress as expected. Nobody could have foreseen then what the impact of the Maruti would be and how India's transport scene – and the whole industrial scene – would be totally transformed in the next twenty years.

Another sign was the increasing reference in the press to a man called Bhindranwale, an emerging leader in the growing tensions in the Punjab...

Impossible dreams

Two of the many who wondered about India's future at the end of the 1970s, and nursed impossible dreams, were M. C. Mathew ('MC') and Anna, his wife. Both doctors, they were working at Sevagram, the community founded by Mahatma Gandhi in Central India and still a centre for social action.

When we first met, MC was wearing *khadi*, the symbol of his Gandhian ideals.

'He wore *khadi* at our wedding,' said Anna. 'This was quite unusual for a Kerala wedding, where clothes are a major item of expense.'

Anna came from a well-established Syrian Christian family in Pune. She trained at the CMC Hospital in Vellore, and met MC at student conferences, where they were both active in a movement among medical students and doctors. At Sevagram, Mathew's Gandhian ideals could be realised. But he didn't start that way.

'As a young student I ignored the reality of God. I thought I could find my way. Then came a phase in my life when I began to see suffering, and I used a Marxist model to respond.'

He became involved in student agitation, and was at the forefront of several student demonstrations. But seeing that protests often lead to aggression, he began to question whether violence was the answer. 'That is when I began to read John's Gospel, where I saw something of the significance of Christ's teaching of inner freedom. And I saw Gandhi as one who used inner freedom, to a certain extent, to bring about consequences. So I was fascinated by Gandhi and studied him for fifteen years of my life, while I also passionately followed the teaching of Jesus Christ.'

Tragedy struck when their second child, Anita Susan, was born with severe difficulties and died at four months. They were devastated by her loss, but also profoundly changed. They saw her as a person created in God's image, as 'a gift of God's love ... her warm and open response to our love made us aware that she was indeed "fully alive", able to touch us deeply with her smiles and sounds.'

As they reflected on their own sadness, they became aware that there was little or no help available for other parents of children like Anita Susan. Caring for children with mental or physical difficulties was hard enough in general. But nobody could do anything for children under seven, it seemed. The parents must wait in despair, confusion or apathy, until the children were older. By then precious opportunities to help them had been lost, sometimes irretrievably.

MC and Anna realised that if anything were to be done, they would have to do it themselves. Developmental Paediatrics was just beginning as a sub-speciality in Europe and America. In India it was inconceivable. With help and encouragement from others they started the Child

Development and Research Centre in 1983 in a small room in Madras. They had 'no equipment, no income, no children or parents coming to them and several inches of water on the floor and courtyard in the monsoon rains'. Other institutions seemed unable or unwilling to help, because the task seemed impossible.

In 1985 they established a Trust called *Ashirvad* (Blessing). The small trickle of parents coming to them began to increase. In 1997 Ashirvad signed an agreement with the Christian Medical College and Hospital at Vellore to begin a new Developmental Paediatrics Unit.

The CMC Hospital was founded in 1900, as a one-bed clinic for women. It is still in the same location, right in the centre of Vellore, near the bus stand. Like any medium-sized town, the streets outside are crowded with the usual procession of people, cows, dogs, pigs, hand-carts, rickshaws, cars, trucks and buses, and the usual noises of horns, bells, shouting, diesel engines and loudspeakers. The hospital grounds are also crowded and busy. This is a 2,000-bed hospital, one of the premier research and teaching institutes in the country. There are 55 clinical departments and new specialities are being added all the time. The campus is packed with buildings, with a continuous process of construction and reconstruction. Everywhere there are people – patients, staff, relatives, doctors, nurses, lab technicians, students – all moving in efficient and purposeful streams. An average 30,000 people pass through the hospital every day. It is a place of healing and service, compassion and hope – but not exactly quiet and beauty. Until you step into the Ashirvad Floor, where the new Developmental Paediatric Unit is based.

It is an oasis of calm and quiet. Posters and pictures smile out at you from the walls. The clean floors are covered with bright and cheerful linoleum. There are toys and books, with chairs and tables at children's level. Everything is geared to be child – and parent – friendly.

Ashirvad's motto is 'Taking Sides'. It stands for a philosophy based on a whole new approach to children with special needs.

> Some say I am a Mongol.
> You call me a Down's Syndrome child
> But I am Jyoti.

Jyoti's picture on the wall is a reminder that she, and any other child, is a unique person, made in God's image. People call children like her 'handicapped' or 'disabled', but Ashirvad thinks of them as children with special needs.

Small beginnings

When Ashirvad began in Madras, only a few parents came, distressed and sometimes despairing, bringing children with a range of difficulties from Down's Syndrome to cerebral palsy, from learning problems to neurological disorders. The parents didn't know what to do, nor did the doctors they consulted. In many cases the child would simply lie in bed or in a corner, without stimulation or hope.

There are at least 5 million children in India with special needs in areas of mental health, learning disabilities and related problems. That is a large number! But compared to other, apparently more pressing needs, it can seem insignificant. In any case, in 1985 there appeared to be no hope of help or treatment for infant children.

MC and Anna began by working with the parents, helping them to understand their child and become involved in his or her development. They introduced creative play-based activities through which children and families could be stimulated and developed. They spent time in supporting the parents and giving them hope.

But this was not just play and sympathy. Each consultation involved meticulous observation. The diagnoses were based on careful research. Ashirvad itself became a source of pioneering research and treatment. Parents were given training and support, so that they could be closely involved with their children's treatment. Suggestions were made for changes in the children's environment at home or school, in diet, nutrition and social activities. The children's physical, mental and emotional development was carefully monitored. In everything the focus was on the child and its well-being. '"A child is at the centre of our attention," and so we make the environment "child friendly and learning friendly".'

A visitor to Ashirvad described what he saw:

> Each little child was special. A long and detailed interview which helped to make an accurate diagnosis of the child's condition was followed by this highly skilled doctor lying on the floor playing with his little patient, while observing her every movement. The parents were thus encouraged to realise that they could play their part by doing likewise at home. Equally impressive, on our last visit, were the enormous strides taken in medical research. Ashirvad is at the forefront of India's research in this field.

The results have been impressive, as families have been changed. It has not usually been a 'cure' because many children's needs are long-term, even 'incurable'. But families have been given hope as they have learned all the positive things they can do. In some cases there have been qualitative improvements in the child's condition. In almost every case they have learned to accept and relate to their child as a person, and to gain a new understanding of God's love and care even through their experience of suffering.

> Parents of a child with multiple needs can find themselves initially overburdened as they make frequent visits to their

doctor and to various specialists, each dealing with a different aspect of the problem. Often they receive what seems to be contradictory advice. Either they refuse to believe the child has special needs and do little to stimulate the child, or else they are overwhelmed by the enormity of the child's need and they struggle on feeling hopeless and helpless – physically and emotionally drained and often socially isolated.

At Ashirvad parents found a place where they were given time – for meticulous and professional examination, for listening to their anxieties, for receiving clear and helpful information:

> One of the things we are most grateful for is the all-round approach. They don't just tackle the health or physical needs of our daughter, but her all-round development as an individual. An equal amount of time is spent on counselling us parents, not only in equipping us to deal with the problems, but also encouraging us to speak out, unburden and share our feelings which has a healing effect on us and we are better able to care for our daughter. Dr Mathew also takes the time to pray with us, covering the spiritual aspect of our needs as well. Kanya loves her visits to Ashirvad. She never feels she is just going for a check-up, but rather for a wonderful treat – an exciting place with lots of fun things to do.

Instead of putting the children into an institution, the Ashirvad approach is to work with the parents, making the most of India's traditional strength of family and community.

Ashirvad's contribution

Ashirvad determined to remain small. This enabled it to maintain quality, give time and keep it personal. Instead of growing large, it encouraged others to develop their own projects, for example Early Learning Centres in Nagpur, Chennai, Valathi (Tamil Nadu), and other places.

Recognition was very slow at first. Were they doing more than playing with a few children and reassuring a few parents? Was there a place for medical people to be involved? Over the years the Centre in Madras became known as a centre of academic excellence in the field, providing services for patients from all over India. A closer link with a teaching institution seemed to be the way to bring care for special children into the medical curriculum. In 1995, after several years of discussion, the CMC Hospital invited Ashirvad to set up a new department. The Development Paediatric Unit would be a fully-fledged speciality like any others. The move took place in 1997. While maintaining its distinctive personal and intimate atmosphere, the new department grew rapidly. In November 1999 a national workshop on 'Neurodevelopmental Issues in Early Childhood' attracted 113 national and international participants. MC hopes soon to have doctors doing their PhD research under him, so that they can become qualified in this new field, the first of their kind in India.

In a quite different sphere, a Tamil Nadu film producer recently made a film, 'Anjali', in which the central character is a child with special needs. It has done a lot to dispel the widespread feeling that a disabled child is a sign of God's disfavour or the result of *karma*. He spent several days observing children at Ashirvad in order to make the film.

MC and Anna see Ashirvad's contribution as a **chain reaction**.

> The challenge to us, as we have received children and their parents, was how to discern God's activity in their lives ... We joined with them in their journey ... and as a result they were able to rediscover value and blessedness in what they were going through. They in turn have become enriched to give themselves to others.

One family with a severely disabled child is now helping to look after fifteen other families in their neighbourhood.

It is also a **two-way process**, in which Ashirvad staff receive as well as give. As they share what they can with families in need, they are inspired and encouraged themselves. 'The parents and children become our educators. They are the text book from whom we learn to move into new directions and new understanding.'

Does Religious Conversion have a place?

What place, if any, does religious conversion have in all this? MC and Anna see their life and work as 'a journey to the truth in which we affirm people and invite them to share their life with us'. Their desire is to 'love and care for them as they are loved and cared for by God', and to help them 'discover the beauty and richness of their life before God'. Often families ask for prayer after the consultation. They pray for them and invite them to join with them in prayer, in order to 'move towards this silent encounter with a loving God'.

We involve ourselves in people's stories … I think the most important event in the last 15–17 years has been seeing people take a turn in the course of their lives, when they were frustrated and questioning, finding hope, meaning, direction and a sense of purpose …

MC believes that Jesus offers abundant life: 'A personal relationship with God is central to our faith, then upbuilding … then helping people to live a holistic life, in a relationship with Christ, in a relationship with their fellow beings … We cannot separate ourselves from people …' In his own experience, that personal relationship is what inspires him and makes the difference.

He had not found this adequately in Gandhiji's way, which he had followed so actively for fifteen years.

Gandhi had a tremendous advantage in that he used peaceful ways and he made prayer the centre of his life. He used methods that would help others also to be part of this change. But what was not sufficient was that there was no spontaneous inner momentum in those who became part of his political system, because they had no personal encounter with a personal God. Ultimately our rootedness in God is what really matters.

Why has Gandhiji's legacy gone? It was based on a principle, without an on-going personal relationship to sustain it. Once Gandhiji himself had gone, his followers were not able to sustain the principle.

Reflection

A counter-cultural movement

The focus at Ashirvad is undoubtedly on inner, spiritual transformation. Yet the element of social and cultural critique is equally strong. Ashirvad and its founders have taken a definite stand as a counter-cultural movement.

Ashirvad 'takes sides' with the marginalised. It has consciously struggled, all through its existence, to remain small, to identify with those whom society finds hard to accept, to affirm their difference and their right to recognition. The struggle has sometimes been hard and has sometimes led to painful misunderstanding. To be different, and yet to be part of the mainstream, is always difficult. But that is precisely the struggle of those with special needs, whom Ashirvad seeks to identify with.

Those who come in contact with Ashirvad, as parents, children, staff or other professionals, soon become aware of this difference. Some may be challenged to discover its source. And that may lead in turn to change in their own personal life and their spiritual understanding and commitment.

Others working with special needs

Of course Ashirvad is only one of many hundreds of organisations in India working with people with special needs. Each has its own story of effort and care, tragedy and triumph. I have met a few of them.

In a Delhi suburb **Rajinder Johar** lies stretched out on his bed. He has been paralysed for the last ten years after a shooting accident in Ludhiana. His brother comes every day to help him wash and dress. For two years after his accident Rajinder was sunk in despair, wondering if it was worth going on living. He met some friends from the Cheshire Home in South Delhi, whose care and concern gave him hope. A year later he was inspired to start the **Family of Disabled (FOD)**, an organisation for people with severe physical disabilities. They publish a newsletter, help each other to find job opportunities, collect information about disability and raise public awareness that the disabled are not rejects but people who are 'differently able'.

At the southern tip of India, a few miles inland from Kanya Kumari, 25 acres of barren land have been turned into forest and fertile farmland. The **Nambikkai Foundation** offers hope to adult deaf people (*nambikkai* means 'hope' in Tamil). Many would find it difficult, if not impossible, to be anything but a burden to their families. At Nambikkai they get training for life skills and employment. **Ian Stillman**, the co-founder, is profoundly deaf from a boyhood illness. In 1976 he rode his Triumph motorcycle from England to India, along with his friend, David Matthews. In Madras he met **Yesumani (Su)**, a teacher in the deaf school. They got married and soon afterwards started the Nambikkai project. It was a hard struggle: establishing the farm, constructing the buildings, finding the right staff, continuing to encourage their trainees when things didn't go well for them.

Other organisations work with the blind, with leprosy patients, with street children, prostitutes, HIV and AIDS victims. Some are large and thriving, some are small and struggling.

All of them are trying to make a difference in an India where economic progress is accelerating but the weaker struggle even more to keep up. They are trying to answer the challenge that MC Mathew throws out, to seek an 'intense, personal transformation and spiritual renewal, as a result of which people are surprised by the way you live'.

7
'Your Passion for These People':
Tribal Transformation in Orissa

> I have taken on your passion for these people. I will come back here.
> — *Iris Paul*

> What might be the link between the struggle for basic rights and the adoption of ... minority religions? What limitations of secular ideologies in ensuring these rights do acts of conversion reveal?
> — *Gauri Viswanathan*

Until the super-cyclone struck in October 1999, few people had given much thought to Orissa. Neither north nor south, overshadowed culturally by its Bengali neighbour, it was a state you passed through on the way to Calcutta, or visited for its beaches and temples.

In addition to the appalling devastation, the cyclone revealed Orissa's poverty and lack of infrastructure. Paradoxically, it is rich in resources with vast mineral deposits, a range of forest products, and exports of rice. But the majority of producers in the state don't earn enough to be able to purchase. 50% are illiterate; 29% are tribals or dalits. Moneylenders are active. Infant mortality is high. Starvation deaths were reported in Kalahandi district in 1998, though that district was actually exporting rice at the time, having gone through its own 'Green Revolution'. (Starvation deaths are generally very rare because few people actually die of starvation; they usually die of something else, made worse by their weakened condition).

In Ganjam district the rich forests are being destroyed. 'Nobody cares for the people' said Hari Krishna of *Gram Vikas*, an organisation that works with poor communities to help them organise against the moneylenders. In the coastal areas aquaculture is the latest big business. Rich investors, many from outside the state, have built up large-scale intensive prawn farms. The effect has been devastating for the local fishermen, who have been excluded from this new industry. They can't afford two meals a day, or enough clothes to wear. It has also disturbed the ecological balance. The Chilikh Lake has receded, and the intensive farming destroys other fish species. In May 1999, 37 people were killed in the 'Chilikh Prawn Riots' as local people protested.

In Balasore district the mangrove trees along the coast have been removed to make way for the prawn tanks. So the natural defences had gone when the cyclone struck, and the floodwaters poured inland, devastating 10,000 square miles of crops. 'It was not the cyclone that killed you, but your poverty and your ignorance,' said one of the community workers.

It was a simple telephone directory that brought home Orissa's poverty to me. In Delhi and Mumbai the phone book comes in two massive volumes, each 4-5 cm thick. In Orissa the phone book for the entire state (population 37.5 million) is a single volume just 1.5 cm thick.

Malkangiri

Malkangiri District, the southernmost in Orissa, is undistinguished. But it is home to one of my most remarkable friends. When I first met Iris she was a medical student at the Kilpauk Medical College in Madras. Some years later I heard that she had married a veterinary doctor, Paul, who was working in a remote part of Orissa. Twenty years after our first meeting, I visited Dr Iris Paul in Malkangiri, in 1992. I travelled there with a friend: it was a thirty-hour train journey from Delhi to Vizianagram in Andhra Pradesh. We arrived in the early morning to find that the buses were on strike. We managed to hitch lifts in two trucks as far as Jeypore, where we were able to hire a taxi. The road took us through deep valleys, surrounded by teak and hardwood forests, across streams and rivers, past fields. In mid-afternoon we reached Malkangiri, a sleepy town with low buildings, dusty brown streets, and small wooden shops. Everything was brown and muddy in the monsoon. Iris lived in a dark, untidy house near the centre. The front room was piled with boxes of medicines, books and papers. There was another room where we ate, then the kitchen and bedrooms, with bathroom and toilet across the small back courtyard.

Iris had lived in Malkangiri since 1972, working along with her husband. But in 1986 he died after a long struggle with kidney disease, innumerable complications and finally heart failure. She was left with four children, two of them adopted. Everybody assumed that she would return to Madras, to the security of her parents' home and the opportunities of a doctor's work. But Iris had told her husband before he died, 'I have taken on your passion for these people. I will not stay in Madras. I will come back here. I promise you, I will come back to Malkangiri and work here to the day I die.'

What was the passion she had inherited?

Paul first came to Malkangiri in 1967, leaving his work as a veterinary doctor in southern Tamil Nadu to join the Indian Missionary Society. He wanted to serve the local people by sharing with them the Good News of Jesus, which he had experienced in his own life. Over half the people of the district were Adivasi tribals. The majority were Koya, and there was a sizeable minority of Santhalis, refugees from Bangladesh who had been resettled in the area by the Government. The most remote group were the Bondo, living in inaccessible villages right up in the hills.

It took Paul a long time to be accepted by the Koya, as he tried to make friends and understand their situation. It was three years before any would talk to him freely. Because he was an outsider they assumed that he had come to exploit them. Their experience with outsiders, whether government officials, traders or moneylenders, had not been happy. Being illiterate and unable to count beyond twenty, they were easily cheated when they sold or bartered their produce. Many lost their land, by pledging it as security for loans that carried enormous interest payments. Alcoholism and poor hygiene meant that there was little prospect of life improving. The men worked sporadically in their fields. Sometimes they spent weeks drinking home-made liquor. Paul shared with them how Jesus could answer their prayer and change their lives from the inside. He also helped them, when they went to the market, to get a fair price from the traders. He prayed with those who were sick.

Gradually Paul saw change in the lives of some of the people, especially a man called Podhiya, who had been the first Koya to speak to him. They wanted to hear more about Jesus. Some wanted to follow Jesus.

In 1972 Paul married Iris. Her father was Chief Engineer of Tamil Nadu and the builder of several of India's big dams. Iris had been brought up in Delhi and Madras and had done exceptionally well in her medical studies. Despite her sophisticated background, she quickly adjusted to the very different lifestyle of Malkangiri and soon found her medical skills in great demand. Paul and Iris were welcome in the Koya villages and one night they were received into the family *(mapsath)* of a village called Thamsa.

> When the Koyas want to take an outsider as a complete member of their own society, they invite you for a feast in the night. They did this for us; they killed a chicken and cooked a festive meal. Then they sang and danced through the night.
>
> The touching thing for me was that every member of the village, men and women, contributed something to make the feast. One might bring one onion, another a piece of firewood, another a little bit of oil. So each has contributed. This made the statement that every single person welcomed us and wanted us as members of their village. Then after the feast and dance, they sang about us.

They sang about Paul as *Denga Babu*, Mr Tall. They described me as the Fat Lady. They didn't mean any offence. Not everyone gets this privilege.

The Bondo

A quite different challenge came from the Bondo, the most inaccessible of the tribals in Orissa, perhaps in all India. Verrier Elwin, who served for many years among the tribals of India, has celebrated their lifestyle in his book *Bondo the Highlander*. Illiterate, prone to bouts of drunkenness and fighting, they are unpredictable and can be dangerous. It is a truly wild and fearless life. Within the strict tribal morality, young men fight for a wife. Women do all the work while the men hunt with poisoned arrows, drink and look after the babies. Everybody smokes, and drinking is part of life from birth. Their lifespan is short because of malaria, TB, child mortality and murder.

I first heard of the Bondo from Sasi Kumar, who had been a student at Hindustan Bible Institute in Madras, where I was working. He went to Orissa to work with Paul and Iris for a few years, until ill health forced him to leave. Together they developed intermittent contacts with the Bondo. Some of their encounters were hair-raising. Once they were threatened at knifepoint. Iris treated horrific illnesses and wounds.

Slowly they began to make friends. But after a while the contacts with the Bondo were broken off, as Paul himself became seriously ill and battled for his life. In 1986 he died.

Working with the Community

Iris stayed on in Malkangiri, as she had promised, though not without tears. She continued to run a dispensary in the town and began to visit the villages again. She became more aware of the problems that dogged them every day. There was the usual range of health problems. There was a lack of accessible water. And there was the ongoing burden of illiteracy. Iris realised the need to work with the people in community development, doing things together *with* them, rather than simply doing things *for* them. She saw the need to tackle the causes of their problems rather than just dealing with the symptoms, preventing disease and tackling poverty, not just offering medicines or handouts.

I could keep curing the illnesses, but it would be so much better to prevent them in the first place. They need vaccinations, clean water, clean kitchen habits, rehydration salts for children with diarrhoea. These things should not be out of reach.

What motivated Iris was her desire that the village people would experience the love of Jesus, as she had experienced it, and would know his concern for the oppressed and the needy. She wanted to demonstrate that by her actions.

She began with a programme of immunisations, particularly against TB. At the same time she taught basic hygiene. In order to provide water she contacted EFICOR, a Delhi-based development organisation with a well-drilling rig. They had dug a number of wells in other parts of Orissa and she urged them to come to Malkangiri District as well. However, they replied that they were waiting for the right opportunity that would fit into their schedule.

Literacy was the next priority. The first team of literacy workers did not meet with a great response. People didn't feel any need to read and write, and the idea of attending a class didn't seem to attract them. Then she hit on the idea of using short plays and sketches to highlight the familiar problems that people faced with the shopkeepers, traders and moneylenders. When people saw how helpless they were and how reading and counting could make a practical difference, the literacy classes took off. Currently 47 literacy motivators and teachers work in 97 centres across the district.

Iris took us to a two-day conference organised for the literacy workers and some of the new literates. We drove in her battered Ambassador car, stopping several times to fix a puncture or push the car to get it started. The journey provided its own interest: as we drove back to Malkangiri town, we suddenly saw a shadowy white shape by the side of the road. As we turned to look, it melted into the trees. It was a tiger – the first and only tiger that I have ever seen in the wild. (Besides the reclusive tigers, there are bears in the district and plenty of other animals including snakes and leeches, to make life difficult when trying to reach a village in the monsoon.)

What struck me most at the conference was the enthusiasm of the new literates. Their pleasure in being able to read was obvious. Literacy had given them a new sense of dignity and ability and had released their creativity in many unexpected ways.

In 1995 the well-drilling rig finally arrived. In some ways the delay proved to be beneficial. Instead of drilling the five wells that Iris had originally asked, the engineers stayed in the area for two years and drilled 300 wells. They were able to build on the network of contacts and relationships that Iris had built up as she worked with the communities. So the communities were involved in the decisions about where to locate a particular well, who would have access to its water, and how to maintain it. By contrast, in nearby Kalahandi District, which has also been transformed by irrigation, only the rich have benefited.

The people now had reliable drinking water, which made a difference to their health and the quality of their daily life. The next step was water resource management, to make best use of water from the wells and from the monsoon rain, which often ran away without being fully used. EFICOR provided water engineers, and the village leaders agreed to work with them to build a small dam at a place called Gottenpalli. It would provide water for a network of irrigation channels. In addition, they built a series of 'gully plugs': small stone barriers that would check the flow of water rushing down the monsoon streambeds. This held the water longer so that more would seep into the ground. It also helped to prevent soil erosion. The villagers worked hard all through the summer and completed their preparations just in time for the monsoon. The results next year were dramatic. The field that had produced four bags of rice now produced forty. It was well worth the effort!

Along with these outward signs of change, people were experiencing inner, spiritual transformation. They were gaining new understanding of God's care and concern, of prayer being answered, of inner peace and forgiveness. Many of the villages now focused their devotion on Jesus and wanted to become his followers. They met to pray and to study the Bible, which many of them could now read.

Exploitation?

In recent years many people have questioned the work being done by missionaries like Iris among tribal people. Are they exploiting them and taking advantage of them?

It is perfectly true that tribal people are under pressure and that their way of life is disappearing. Verrier Elwin, the missionary turned anthropologist, spent most of his life living with tribal people in different parts of India. He felt passionately that they should be left alone to preserve their way of life, or to choose a different way, on their own. But this is not happening. 'Civilisation' is constantly pressing on the tribals, squeezing them every day into smaller and smaller confines. Dams and factories flatten hundreds of square kilometres of forest and uproot thousands of people from their land. Business and agriculture encroach on their space. Arundhati Roy has recently highlighted the problems caused by the relentless pressure of 'urban', 'modern' India, symbolised especially in the Narmada Dam project. A friend heard her give the Jawaharlal Nehru Memorial Lecture at Cambridge University, which she called *The Cost of Living*. He recorded some of the comments in the hot debate that followed her lecture:

During the course of the debate her crusade got naturally linked with the Pope's recent call for evangelisation (November 1999).

A student of Development Economics reacted to the Pope's call with the typical Liberal argument: 'Why do these missionaries have to disturb the cultures of the tribals? They have lived happily for thousands of years, why don't they leave them alone?'

An Environmentalist challenged him: 'Has anything disrupted the culture and lifestyle of the tribals more than the development plans of secularists like you? Don't your dams, roads, and railway lines destroy the Eco-systems on which their lifestyle has been dependent for ages? Aren't your development plans the single biggest factor throwing the tribals out of their jungles into the slums of urban India? You Liberals have destroyed the indigenous cultures at least as much as anyone else.'

Another student asked: 'By the way, how do you know that the tribals are happy as they are? On what basis do you assume that those tribals may not want their children to have the option of studying in Cambridge? Would you like to live as your forefathers always lived? Should the mission schools educate only the elite of India enabling them to get scholarships from the Nehru Memorial Trust to come here and go back to build those dams that destroy indigenous cultures?'

A fourth student critiqued both the Liberal and the Environmentalist: 'Arundhati Roy was brilliant; but her crusade is at best a First Aid. Is it enough to stop these dams and let the marginalised continue to exist at the level of subsistence, without an opportunity to develop their minds and creativity through education, self-respect, and new forms of organisations?

'The Pope is right: they will never have the option to develop themselves and make their full contribution to their nation and the world, unless someone goes to them with the dedication of a missionary to educate and empower them. To be empowered is to have options. If they are content with their situation then there is nothing to fear. They would reject new ideas, beliefs and values, but isn't it cruel to deny them the possibility of options?'

One of the saddest stories in Mark Tully's book *No Full Stops In India* is his meeting with Gond tribals near the place where Verrier Elwin dedicated many of his best years in service. The former tribal leader whom he met had lost much of his culture and even more of his dignity through his assimilation to mainstream, modern, Indian culture. He was sustained now by alcohol and handouts. But the only option Mark Tully could suggest was a return to the old tribal life, which may have been simple but was hardly idyllic. Are there no other options? Is there no way of helping tribals to move from the severe limitations and degradation of their present situation, without losing their dignity or the attractive features of their tribal community life?

In Malkangiri I saw people like Iris extend practical help based on compassion, to give the tribals new options – health care, clean water and improvements in agriculture – that were genuinely liberating. She and her colleagues worked *with* the people, involving them in all the decisions. Some of them also opted to identify themselves with the new spiritual dimension that they observed. They experienced personal change that enabled them to overcome old habits and sustain new values.

Reflection : The Questions Still Remain

Doesn't religious conversion take away people's culture and produce conflict?

That may be true in certain cases. As we have seen, conversion is by definition an unsettling experience, both for those who opt for change and for the rest of their community. It is made worse when people are taught to reject all their past, instead of discerning what was good and what needed to be changed.

But I saw no attempts to change local customs. Of course, changes were going on all the time, for better and for worse, through contact with the mainstream of the wider world. So people were having to make choices as they responded to those external changes, some welcome, some thrust on them.

How people respond to change is an issue that keeps coming up and we will return to it again.

But why work with the poor?

Why not work with others who are better-educated and less in danger of manipulation or exploitation?

The short answer might be: *Why not?* When people are clearly marginalised and disadvantaged, why not seek to help and serve them? Does it need any further justification?

A longer answer is: the good news of God's love and the transformation that can come from it is not just for the poor, but for people of every social and cultural background. Those who are better off materially have less obvious needs. But their need for inner peace, for freedom from selfishness and greed, for contentment and compassion, may be even greater.

The challenge for all of us is to realise that material well-being is not enough. There is always a danger of thinking that economic and social improvements alone are the goal. When I first came back to India, that was where I was tempted to focus. Of course, they are vital. People are whole beings. We all need to eat and be clothed. *And* we need to know God, the source of our being and all that we have and are. Jesus said, 'Man shall not live by bread alone, but by every word that comes from the mouth of God' (The New

Testament, Gospel of Matthew, 4.4). He was indicating that *both* sides of our humanity are important. The physical and spiritual both need feeding.

Iris and her colleagues saw no separation between caring for people's obvious physical needs, working with them for justice and *also* sharing with them their own experience of spiritual transformation.

The question for those of us who are not poor is: how are we using our talents and privileges – not just for ourselves, but also for others? Iris gives a model of caring and sharing, serving and equipping. Follow that model and you soon find that you need inner, spiritual resources to keep going. You need somebody to inspire you, somebody to give you the power.

But doesn't religious conversion weaken political loyalty and lead to unrest and even independence movements? What about the troubled states of the North East? That is our next question.

8
Neglected Sisters: The Riddle of the North-east

The problem of religious minorities continues to be one of the most vexing and intriguing problems of contemporary India.

— *Shripaty Sastri*

We were brought into contact with the outside world by Christianity ... It is not an isolating factor, as is sometimes charged.

— *Leno Terhuja*

Blaming the 'inherent separatism' or similar 'ills' of the NEHA tribes upon such favourite whipping horses as ... 'activities of foreign missionaries' only helps in diverting attention from identifying the real factors responsible for weak integration.

— *M. N. Srinivas*

6 December 1992. It was the day after the destruction of the Babri Masjid in Ayodhya, and most of India was still in shock. I was travelling on a half-empty train from Delhi to Calcutta, on my way to Mizoram. Many passengers had cancelled their journeys and those of us left were an anxious group. We were even more anxious when our train stopped

at Patna and the loudspeaker announced that we would remain there indefinitely. But after a few hours we began moving again and reached Calcutta early next morning. Howrah Station had just reopened after twenty-four hours curfew, and with great difficulty I got a taxi to the airport. More chaos, as many flights had been cancelled. In the queue I was relieved to recognise a Mizo friend, also on his way to Mizoram. Four hours later we found ourselves on the flight to Silchar, in Assam. We arrived just before dusk and were packed into two minibuses, in a great rush because a curfew had been announced. In the confusion I was separated from my friend. The general sense of nervousness turned to anxiety as our minibus stopped with a puncture. By the time we got moving again it was dark. We reached the town in pitch blackness. Anxiety was now fear, as rumours were spreading about 'shoot at sight' orders.

I finally reached my friend at the Mizoram guesthouse. But our relief at getting safely *into* Silchar was replaced the next morning by concern about how to get *out*, as there was a ban on road transport. Suddenly a government vehicle arrived from somewhere for one of the Mizos and we quickly left, hoping we would not be stopped. Within half an hour we had crossed the state border into Mizoram and began to relax. We were into the hills, where there was a different perspective on events in the plains.

I reflected that the tension and fear of my journey must have been like the feelings of many earlier outsiders to the region. But in their case they were afraid of what might happen when they got *into* the hills, with their fierce and reclusive tribal inhabitants.

Isolation

Northeast India is a different world, isolated by

geography, culture and politics. Two hundred years ago the plains of Assam consisted of several Hindu kingdoms. The tribal hunters of the hills lived in thousands of independent villages, perched on the top of hills, guarded by night and day, separated from other villages by valleys. Their only contact with the outside world of the plains was occasional raids, or visits to barter their crops in exchange for salt and other provisions. In 1826 the East India Company signed the Treaty of Yandabo with the King of Burma, in which he relinquished his claim to the region, enabling the Company to claim it themselves. Their motive, of course, was economic, and the most significant product of the region soon became tea, especially as the tea trade with China became uncertain.

The British left the hill tribes alone at first but inevitably their power spread, especially out of annoyance at the occasional raids. The Lushai Hills, for example, were annexed in response to increasing raids by the Lushai (Mizo) hunters on the spreading tea plantations below.

Almost from the beginning, the British maintained the isolation of the hill people. The Inner Line Regulation of 1873 restricted the right of outsiders to enter the hill areas to live, work or buy property. Its purpose was to protect the tribals' way of life but it also kept them separate. In 1932 the hill areas were again designated as either 'Excluded Areas' (roughly corresponding to Nagaland, Mizoram, Arunachal Pradesh, Manipur and some parts of Assam) or 'Partially Excluded Areas' (Meghalaya and other parts of Assam). In all the ferment of the pre-Independence years, the whole area was excluded from the changes taking place in the rest of India. K. S. Singh comments that 'for most tribes in North-eastern hill areas the experience of being integral parts of a nation is relatively recent'.

After independence the cultural and political isolation was reinforced by a new geographical separation, as East Pakistan was carved out between the North East and the rest of India. Only a narrow corridor connects West Bengal with Assam and, through that, the other six states into which it has been divided. Getting there means a minimum of sixteen hours by train or bus, if you can't afford to fly. In either case you then need to travel several more hours by bus, jeep or on foot.

Diversity

Diversity is the second surprise of North-east India. From the outside you think of it as one region, 'the North-east' or 'Assam' (like calling all South Indians 'Madrasis'). But each part is very different from the other. In an area smaller than Andhra Pradesh, there are 209 scheduled tribes and over fifty major language groups. There are sharp divisions between the hills and plains. The people are descended from waves of invasions and migrations from Tibet, China, South East Asia and more recently from West Bengal and Bangladesh. The 'Seven Sisters' have recently been joined by Sikkim as the eighth state in the North Eastern Council.

So generalisations about the region need to be made with caution. My personal experience of being there is limited to a couple of weeks each in Shillong and Aizawl, very different places. While I have many friends, colleagues and former students from the region, I have worked most closely with Mizos.

Mizo Professionals

The North East has a large proportion of professionals, serving not only in their own states but also across India, several in high-calibre government posts. Lalchuangliana was an Assistant Collector in Gwalior District, whom I met in 1971 while visiting a friend from student days, who had also joined the IAS (Indian Administrative Service) in Madhya Pradesh. Lalchuangliana had been a teacher before he applied for the IAS. He recalled how in his village development had been comparatively recent. Children starting school might have no record of their birth. The headmaster would look at them, assess their ages and assign them a birth date – often 1 January, a good day for a birthday! Or sometimes the assigning of birth dates happened when students were preparing for the Matriculation exams and had to fill in a form for the official records. 'Our teachers filled the forms without bothering to ask the students their exact birth dates and they simply filled the dates as either January 1 or March 31 (the end of the school year)'.

Three years later I met Lalchuangliana again in Delhi. He had left his promising career to join an NGO (non-governmental organisation) specialising in health care. Emmanuel Hospital Association (EHA) had, at that time, about twenty hospitals and community health programmes across north India. Keeping the projects running was a formidable task. It involved dealing with the varying, sometimes conflicting, needs of over 1,000 staff, recruiting quality doctors and nurses to work in very remote rural areas, raising the necessary finances to provide care for poorer patients, and handling legal disputes. His administrative experience enabled him to provide the 'steel frame' that kept EHA going, and expanding, through the 1970s and 1980s. His calm, unflappable exterior concealed his fervent desire to serve God and the people of North India.

Dr Nghakliana, another Mizo, resigned from medical practice to work with students in North India. Based in Lucknow, he and his wife had an open home where students of all backgrounds were welcome, to receive friendship and counsel, or to study the Bible together. Nghakliana died suddenly of cancer in 1985. The following year his younger brother, L. N. Tluanga, arrived in Delhi with his wife, Biaki. Shoko and I met them at a conference and we quickly became friends. Five years later we were posted to Delhi and worked together with them for two years. Tluanga had been Director of Education in the Government of Mizoram. With several years' service ahead of him, he surprised everybody by resigning to go to Kiribati, a remote group of islands in the Western Pacific, almost on the International Dateline (the Kiribati islanders were among the first to welcome the new millennium). Tluanga and Biaki served in a mission school for five years before returning to India to work with an educational charity. When we joined them in Delhi, he had been appointed general secretary of another NGO. His breadth of experience and his wise and gracious demeanour earned him respect and affection everywhere. When their daughter-in-law died suddenly of cancer, Biaki took on the care of their two grandsons, aged four and two, no small task at an age when they were preparing to retire. When they did retire they returned briefly to Mizoram, only to uproot once again for a further term of service in Kiribati.

It was Tluanga who arranged my visit to Aizawl, enabling me to get the necessary permits. Aizawl is a straggling town spread across several hills, with steep, winding roads that curve endlessly round the hillsides, past crowded markets and beautiful views across the hills.

Christianity in Mizoram

When I finally reached there, in December 1992, preparations were under way to celebrate the hundredth anniversary of the coming of Christianity to Mizoram, in

1894. The celebrations included the biggest drum in the world, made from a single buffalo hide stretched over a hollowed-out tree trunk, over six feet wide. Drums have always had a central place in Mizo culture.

In their church meetings the Mizos are solemn and dignified. The music is beautiful, much of it in Western style, until they break into a Mizo tune, and then the whole atmosphere changes, with minor keys and the insistent rhythm of the drums. When Christianity came to Mizoram it encountered strong opposition at first. But as it grew, it adapted to the tribal culture and was careful to maintain it wherever possible. The church plays a major place in Mizo life, asserting strong moral and spiritual influence on society. Today it is concerned with troubling issues like the growing unemployment among young people, the influence of drugs and the impact of corruption. Mizo women have campaigned during some elections, exposing candidates prone to alcoholism or corruption. Mizo housewives set aside a handful of rice every day, as they prepare the family meals. The rice is collected each week and goes to the church, providing a substantial part of the church's budget for its social work and outreach inside and outside Mizoram.

But what has been the impact of Christianity on North Eastern society in general? One perception that has been strong and consistent in many parts of India is this: Christianity is the main cause of the separatist trend in the North East. As recently as October 2000, Jay Lakhani repeats this typical view:

> It has been noticed that in many areas, particularly in the North East, the foreign missionaries have created unhealthy and undesirable elements ... the conversions carried out by the foreign missionaries in the North East have resulted in ... separatist tendencies' (*Asian Voice*, 21 October, 2000).

Ask almost anybody in India and you'll get the same answer:
   The North-eastern people, especially the hill people, feel
   themselves separate from the rest of India. The main cause
   for this is Christianity.

No one will disagree with the first sentence. The
differences are rooted in geography, history and culture. But
what is the link with Christianity? The answer is much more
complex than the common perception.

The Coming of Christianity to North-east India

After the British annexed Assam, the hill areas remained
remote and inaccessible, even when they were nominally
under government control. Missionaries eventually ventured
into the different hill regions, though they did not reach the
Lushai Hills until 1894. Their preaching met with little
response at first. There was considerable hostility to any
change. But two things did make an impact. The Mizos'
highest ideal of character is *tlawmngaihna* – self sacrifice.
It means denying yourself the best share in the feast, giving
up your place by the fire to someone else, or making the
ultimate sacrifice in battle on behalf of your village or clan.
As the Mizos heard about Jesus, they recognised one who
embodied their highest ideals, especially in his death on the
cross. A few years later they also saw this ideal exemplified
in the lives of Christians, during one of the great bamboo
famines. Every few years the bamboo that covers the hills
flowers abnormally. This leads to a plague of rats that destroy
the crops, resulting in famine. At these times the villages that
had escaped the plague would build stockades to keep out
the hungry from other villages. There would be fights and
killing, on top of the plague. But during the famine of 1911–
12 the opposite happened – people were willing to share with
others. It was recognised that this was caused by the impact

of the teaching of Christ and the change it had brought in his followers. From then on Christianity spread rapidly through the whole tribe, resulting in significant changes in literacy, education, health and the role of women.

The pattern was similar in the nearby Naga Hills (now Nagaland and Manipur). But it was much more uneven because of the far greater diversity of the Nagas, with their many different tribes. Even within the same tribe, each village, perched on its hilltop, was an independent republic, with its own democratic leadership, separated by deep valleys and back-breaking climbs from the next. There were often marked differences of language and custom.

By 1947 Christianity was well established in all the hill regions and by 2000 the percentage of Christians in their populations had grown even further (for example Manipur: 34.1%, Meghalaya: 64.6%, Mizoram: 85%, Nagaland: 87.5%). Christianity has permeated every level of society.

But has it been an alien force, detribalising the local culture and fostering separatism?

Cultural Changes

The region certainly went through dramatic changes in the 100–150 year period since Christianity came to its different areas. The early missionaries did seek to change some of the tribal customs that they considered wrong, for moral or other reasons. These included slavery and headhunting (for which they petitioned the government), and certain festivals. Along with this went other practices like the use of drums and the traditional 'dormitories' in which the young men of some tribes lived together. However, many customs related to marriage, inheritance and tribal decision-making were retained. On the positive side came the strengthening of tribal identity as people of different villages and dialects were brought together, with a common script for reading and writing, and common institutions across the tribe. In Assam, missionaries campaigned against the government for the local language, Assamese, and against the imposition of Bengali as the language of government and education. Literacy, education and health care were introduced and the place of women was greatly strengthened. Literacy today is up to 90% in some tribes.

It is a matter of debate how many of these changes were brought through Christianity and how much was due to the influence of the colonial administration. Their roles were sometimes complementary, sometimes in conflict. S. Chaube comments:

> The contribution of the British government may be summed up under the following categories: the establishment of law and order, improvement in communication, introduction of money economy in the remote areas and... the creation of vested interests. The task of acculturation on the subjective level was almost entirely left to the church. (*Hill Politics in North East India*, Orient Longman 1973, p. 42)

The changes in tribal society and culture during the British period were certainly radical. But they took place in comparative isolation from the rest of India. What happened before 1947 seemed to be as nothing compared to the flood of influences that followed Independence.

It was not just the energy and enthusiasm of the new administration. The sensitive border situation meant that when a separatist movement began with the Nagas, it brought strong intervention from the central government. The Indian Army, government officials and development funds all came pouring in, bringing drastic changes and sudden exposure to a combination of modernisation and Indianisation. Roads were built and communications upgraded. Paradoxically, the influx of development money has not resulted in substantial economic investment or a strong infrastructure, but has created an elite class of government employees and contractors. Economic development has lagged behind the rest of India, for a complex range of reasons. Drug abuse has risen sharply, linked to youth unemployment and the continued existence of underground armies that sometimes use drug trafficking to finance their operations.

The last fifty years have seen deep and sometimes traumatic changes. While Christianity was one of the initial agents of cultural and social change, it has also been a strong force for maintaining identity and stability in the face of change.

Separatism?

What about the separatist trend? Throughout the pre-Independence period, as we saw, the hill people remained in comparative isolation. The sense of isolation and difference came to a head after Independence. Not all the people of the North East felt themselves included in the new India, and there have been struggles – many of them violent ones – from 1947 until the present. Even for those who have not joined separatist movements, there has often been a sense of mutual misunderstanding. North Eastern students coming to other parts of India felt they were treated differently, sometimes cheated or mocked. And they felt themselves different from the rest of India: 'He married an Indian', a Naga student once told me about a fellow Naga.

How did separatist movements develop? Once again we have to beware of generalisations about 'the North East'. Different movements have started at different times and for quite distinct reasons.

Naga separatist movements started before Independence

One of my students in Pune explained to me at great length how the Nagas had never been subject to any other power, except briefly when they accepted British rule. They were never part of India, he said, and did not recognise the government that came into being at Independence. He himself had been part of an underground army, training in the jungle and engaging in regular operations against the Indian army, until a severe grenade wound made him rethink his priorities. He realised that violence was not compatible with his Christian faith and he decided to give his life for a different kind of service – hence his entry into theological study. But he still argued that the Nagas really should be independent, even though by then a peaceful political solution had been reached.

The Mizo insurgency began only in the 1960s

It started when the people felt that the government had failed to respond to the severe bamboo famine. The Mizo National Famine Front became the Mizo National Front, a militant group proclaiming independence in 1966. After years of struggle, their leader Laldenga signed a peace accord with Rajiv Gandhi in 1986.

Immigration sparked off separatist movements in Assam, Tripura and Meghalaya in the 1980s

The local people (both hill and plains) felt themselves swamped by large influxes of people, both from other parts of India and from Bangladesh. A series of indigenous movements, some of them violent, were their response.

Today there are still tensions between different tribal groups and between hill and plain people in some parts of the region.

Is Christianity the cause? Clearly many of those involved in separatist movements were Christian, because they were the majority of the population. And some might have used their religious beliefs to support their political and regional agenda. Dr Lalchungnunga, Principal of Serampore College in West Bengal, points out that it is not Christianity as such that brings about 'narrow domestic regional feeling'.

> It is some sort of 'territorialisation' or 'communali-sation' of it that becomes a mobilising factor for Mizo regionalism. Such instances of territorialisation of religion fomenting regional feeling are often seen in other state and national political systems, be it the case of Hinduism or Islam or Buddhism. (Lalchungnunga, 1994, p. 51.)

Many North Eastern people had strong sympathy for the idea of independence, but this was based on a complex combination of historical, geographical and cultural differences. They know today that this is a total impossibility, flying in the face of geopolitical reality. And whatever the origins of each separatist movement, Christians have usually been in the forefront of those seeking a peaceful resolution and mediation in the conflict.

Conclusion

The North East region faces complex problems for which there are no simple solutions. The churches are struggling to help their members cope with these problems and to work with the government and other institutions to meet them. There are no foreign missionaries in any part of North East India (with a few exceptions in the Catholic church). There is no foreign funding of church work. It is supported by the gifts of its members, as we have seen. The problems are caused by the region's isolation, its complex social and cultural diversity, and the rapid changes of the last fifty years.

Without the steadying influence of Christianity, there is no doubt that the problems would be much worse.

'We used to think India was foreign to us', a friend told me. 'In some ways we hated it. But we have learned to love India. We want to share with other Indians the same message of God's love that we have experienced in our society.'

9
Urban Poverty: Different Approaches in the Delhi Slums

The whole of Delhi will become an overcrowded slum
buried under rubbish.

— *Rahul Bedi*

Good people in Delhi have good fortune and we don't
have it, we are poor. And we are meant to be poor ...

— *A slum dweller*

They need God ... if you simply provide means and things
and privileges, they take you for granted.

— *A social worker*

We saw the puppy first, a reddish-brown flash darting
between the grey-black shapes of the pigs. They were moving
back and forth across the rubbish heap, scavenging for
anything they could find. Then we saw another grey shape,
an old woman on the rubbish heap picking up plastic bags
and scraps of paper and cloth.

How many rag pickers are there in a city? How many
rich and poor? How many in between? Like most other
countries, India has experienced explosive urban growth in
the last thirty years, with all its attendant progress and

problems. Sleepy provincial towns have become cities of over one million inhabitants. Old-established cities have become mega-cities, with millions of tons of concrete poured into sky-scraping apartment blocks, commercial complexes, flyovers, factories and acres of housing colonies. The cities produce jobs and opportunities, diversity and excitement, pollution and slums.

Basti, cheri, jhuggi – whatever you call them, slums are a fact of urban life. They make up 28% of Delhi and a similar proportion of every Indian city.

According to one recent report, 'the whole of Delhi will become an overcrowded slum buried under rubbish unless immediate measures to contain pollution, overcrowding, crime and traffic chaos' are implemented. The slums will 'encroach on all available space within two years. 57% of [Delhi's] inhabitants will have no water, 41% no sewerage and 40% no power.' (Rahul Bedi in the *Daily Telegraph*, 14 August 1999)

Delhi residents already know that they can hardly breathe because of pollution and can hardly move because of traffic congestion. The vehicle population increased nine times more than the human population during the 1980s and shows no sign of decreasing.

Urban poverty has many causes. One is the daily influx of people flocking into the city, escaping from the dead-end of rural poverty in search of a better life. Five hundred come into Delhi every day. Some find new opportunities. The majority remain caught in an urban poverty trap. They end up on the pavements or in the slums.

Some slums are well established with brick or concrete buildings. The majority are huts, temporary constructions of thatch, corrugated iron or whatever is available. For years the road from Mumbai's Santa Cruz airport was lined with enormous metal sewage pipes, waiting to be installed in the ground. Whole families lived in each pipe for almost a decade.

Rodrick Gilbert is leader of a church in the Delhi slums. He has worked there for the last five years. He explains what slum houses are like:

> A slum house is a small space covered with a small sheet of metal or cardboard. It may not be big enough to contain a double bed. There is only one room, about the size of the toilet of a good house. The whole family sleeps on the floor. Normally they don't have beds, tables or chairs and there is no bathroom or kitchen, no toilet, no sitting room. There is only one place which they use for everything, and in many houses that's also the place which is used for the kitchen. They cook right there, they eat right there, they sleep right there, and they go out to ease themselves.

Where?

> They just go for the toilet outside of the slum, any place which is vacant, on the roadside, on the side of a drain. There is almost nil civic amenities in the slum.

Curiously, many slum dwellers have a good electricity supply. They simply attach a wire to the overhead cables, paying a monthly fee to the man from the electricity board.

Walking through a slum you pick your way along the narrow alleys between the huts, avoiding animals, children or the pools of dirt.

> They are such small houses and the next house won't be far from this house, it will be wall to wall. And many times the streets are not wider than you can carry a bicycle. You may not be able to overtake a bicycle in these narrow streets. Sometimes you feel you are entering someone's house and that is the street.

It's tolerable when the sun shines – though not when it really

shines. Then it's unbearably hot. But even that is better than
the misery of the monsoon.

Delhi goes down to 2–3°C in winter and rises up to 45–
48°C in summer, so Delhi faces a variation in climate of
40–45°C. People die of heat here. People die of cold. In
the slums there is no protection from straight heat or cold.
Ninety percent of these people are illiterate and because
there is no civic amenities there is a lot of sickness.
Because their dogs and cats are with them, their chickens
are with them, their pigs are with them, their cows –
everything just messes up in the same place where they
live. So they often fall sick. Men usually drink and they
have many more intoxicating habits which drag them
down, so many men don't work. In those cases women
will have to find work doing dishes in houses or doing
floors in houses. This is why slums are situated right in
the posh areas; there are slums around embassies, because
these are people that get work to do in posh colonies.
Women work, children work because the men just drink
and don't really do much.

In Delhi the older houses all had servants' quarters, with
lanes at the back for the servants to use. But the new
apartment blocks don't have them and domestic servants are
recruited from the nearby slums. Each hotel, building site or
apartment block has its cluster of huts nearby.

Slum dwellers are never secure. The land they occupy
doesn't belong to them, so they are always liable to be
moved. Shanta, whose husband was an alcoholic, managed
to rent a few square feet in a 'colony' on disused land. Her
brother-in-law, a carpenter, helped to put up her hut. The man
who rented the space to her does not own it: they are all there
temporarily, relying on his negotiating skills with the 'real'
owner of the land.

In 1976 the bulldozers levelled acres of Delhi *jhuggis*,

as part of Sanjay Gandhi's cleaning up of the city. Gobind was one of thousands forcibly transferred to new sites. Instead of walking a quarter of a mile from his hut, he had to travel for two hours by crowded bus to work each day. The bulldozers may come back any day to clean up the Delhi slums, if a recent Supreme Court Judgement (April 2000) is implemented. In theory the judgement is aimed at land-grabbers and slum landlords. In practice the poor residents suffer, as the police herd them out.

Many slum people are hardworking and enterprising. They have to be, especially the women and children. Many children are rag pickers, scouring the streets and bringing their loads to a central collection point.

Anwar and Naseema are fortunate: Azad, the man who takes their rags, weighs fairly. But children are perhaps the worst sufferers from slum life. There is little time for recreation. Family life is fragmented and can be violent.

Shareen is aged ten. Her arms and legs are scarred with cuts and burns. Home is a crowded hut with nine brothers and sisters. Her days are spent scavenging in the streets and rubbish dumps for paper and plastic, then she works often till late at night. She also works as a domestic cleaner. She will be married by the age of fourteen.

Fatima, another domestic cleaner, already has five children. She often comes to work dizzy from hunger, or beaten by her husband when he is drunk. Pregnant with her sixth child, she simply says, 'It is God's will.'

Where do you begin in response to the needs of the urban poor – or the needs of the city as a whole?

Talking to friends in Delhi, Mumbai and Chennai, I have found various responses.

Monodeep, whom I first met as a student in Pune, had no clear plan when he returned to Delhi and joined the Delhi

Brotherhood Society, a monastic community whose most
famous former member was C. F. Andrews, Mahatma
Gandhi's associate. The members of the Brotherhood serve
the spiritual and social needs of a range of communities in
Old Delhi and East Delhi. Monodeep was attached to a
church in the Trans Yamuna area. Among those who came
were leprosy patients who had migrated from other parts of
India. As the Brotherhood served the leprosy patients' needs,
and particularly cared for the children, other people were
attracted by the care and concern they saw. For Monodeep,
this was a spontaneous response, unplanned by the
organisation: 'We serve people because of the command of
Christ.' They respond because of their 'spiritual encounter
with Jesus Christ'. They had distributed blankets and later
they found that some had passed them on to others who were
even more needy. 'To us that was a sign of their genuineness:
they were ready for baptism.'

Dr Kiran Martin, on the other hand, had very definite
plans when she set up Asha, a community health and
development society, dedicated to 'improving the lives of
slum dwellers in Delhi'.

As you drive through RK Puram, you pass a busy market,
then a line of unusual buildings. Their soft brown brick
contrasts with the usual grey concrete or yellow plaster
buildings. This is Ekta Vihar (Unity Colony). Facing the
street is Asha's clinic and administrative centre, built in a
simple but elegant design. Behind it you step into a collection
of small brick houses, built in the same style and neatly laid
out along brick paved lanes with proper drainage. Adequate
water supply and toilets make it easier for the community to
keep the area clean. Their health is maintained by local
women who have been trained as community health
volunteers.

This used to be a slum like any other, with temporary buildings and unhygienic conditions. Now the community has security on the land and the ability to maintain themselves with dignity.

Asha follows the same approach to community health and development as Dr Arole and others in rural areas. They work with the community, identify felt needs and equip members of the community to tackle them. There is a strong focus on health education and working with women and children to enable them to prevent disease, improve nutrition and find income. One of Asha's significant achievements has been to work also with officials of the various municipal bodies in Delhi. With their co-operation and funding two slum areas have been completely transformed as model housing projects. Ekta Vihar and Shanti Vihar, a parallel project, have provided a model for the city's slum housing policy.

The key is the work that Asha staff have done with community leaders to motivate and equip them to work together. When this is combined with health care and education, and the capital funding to rebuild the slum colony, the results are dynamic. Asha's aim is to show that:

> Legally provided shelter for the urban poor is the key to a sustainable solution to urban poverty. Instead of turning a blind eye to the slums, or bulldozing them out of existence, the solution is to provide a legally recognised alternative with basic amenities.

Others work with *micro-enterprise* development. **Ahmed** is a community leader in a colony beside the Yamuna river. It was flooded one year, burned down another. Ahmed has started a small school for the children of the area. The room is so small that you have to climb over the desks to get in. He has also received small loans of Rs500–Rs1000, which he passes on to members of the community. One used the money to buy a cycle rickshaw; another bought a handcart from which he sells vegetables. Amazingly, most of these micro-loans are paid back within a year – a record that makes banks envious!

Others focus on the needs and opportunities of *children*. In Mumbai several organisations run pavement clubs, in which street children can learn to read and write, have a meal – and have some fun. They have no space in their lives for recreation. They live by their wits, escaping from the harshness of home or the exploitation of other adults.

> It's called the Pavement Club because its only members are Mumbai's street children. It is attached to a small church in a grubby back lane and this week I had the privilege to witness what happens when the club meets. It was one of the more moving experiences of my life ... They sang, they danced, they played with toys and left after being given the only square meal they get in seven days ... The only love ... the only caring ... these children have ever known is what they get every Friday afternoon ... (Tavleen Singh, *India Today*, 22 February 1999)

Sugandh (*Fragrance*) is a charitable society in Delhi that provides education and vocational training for slum children. In a small rented flat in Lajpat Nagar, children from the neighbouring slum gather each morning. They can only spare a couple of hours a day before going to work. The classes teach them to read and write, to express themselves through art and craft. Anwar looks older than his ten years, though physically he is small. He proudly showed me the pictures he had drawn and demonstrated his new ability to read and write. He is also part of a group that is learning screen-printing, to produce beautiful cards and other craft items that sell briskly in Delhi's hotels and embassies. These children's potential is beginning to be realised. And their parents, though initially cautious, are pleased because their children are not being stopped from working but are being given skills that they can use.

Gilbert, the slum church leader, believes that people's basic need is spiritual. At first sight other problems strike you – the overcrowding, the lack of hygiene, the problems of alcoholism, the sheer pressure of life. Gilbert comments:

> They need God. In our experience, if you simply provide means and things and privileges, they take you for granted. In most of the cases they make a fool of you.

One obvious problem is sickness.

> There is a lot of sickness: people have coughs or asthmatic diseases during the winter. The same people are sick of heat through the summer, or sick of epidemics during the rainy season, when the whole mess rots in there. I mean there is no sickness-free season for them.
>
> Once they are sick, because of their low educational standard, they feel that there is a demonic curse, or something from God. So they go for a divine treatment which is given by a witch doctor in the community. This doctor is usually a temple priest or somebody who does witchcraft. He is essentially a person who is demon possessed. He can read palms and tell their fortunes. When they go to him, he will place demands before them: they must give him three chickens or five chickens, so much of wine and so much of money. He tells them 'I will have to perform this worship or that worship to get rid of this for you.' It might just be a malaria or pneumonia. The people would have to bring a lot of stuff just to get one amulet or some charm or something. He would perform and give it to them, and they stay sick.
>
> The sicknesses are contagious many times. They are passed on from neighbour to neighbour, from members to members in the family.

This puts the thought in their hearts that God is not happy with them, he is not giving them good fortune. 'Good people in Delhi have good fortune and we don't have it, we are poor. And we are meant to be poor because of our deeds in the past and in our previous life. So we are meant to stay the same.

This is their worldview and this is why people have low self-esteem and they have no vision to come out of the community or situation.

Gilbert's approach is based on prayer and counselling. The members of his church offer to pray for those who are sick. Most people welcome this, as it is free, and they are open to spiritual help from any direction. Along with prayer the church members provide counselling and invite people to join a small cell group. This is a group in which up to eight local families meet together regularly, based in one of the local slum colonies. In the group people find mutual support and encouragement. They can continue to pray and study the Bible, where they learn more about God and the teaching of Jesus, and find spiritual answers to the practical issues of daily life. Many of them decide to become followers of Christ, receiving his forgiveness and praying for his guidance and control in their lives.

For many this brings profound change. They are released from their fears and have a sense of acceptance and worth, in place of their former feelings of guilt and doubt. They experience the presence of Christ as a living saviour, friend and guide.

This inner change results in many other changes in their daily lives. Gilbert believes this takes place best as people watch others:

The key is modelling. It is our experience that people learn more by seeing than by hearing. My house personally is

open for everybody. I always have a number of people
coming. The house is open for them to stay. People come
and they stay and live with us. Since the beginning we
have always had people come and stay with us. They saw
our standard and how we live. Then they went back and
changed their lifestyle because they saw us.

What kind of changes?

They began to stay clean, they began to clean their houses,
bathe properly and cook properly. They stopped drinking
and smoking and they stopped going to witch doctors.
They whitewashed their houses, they washed their clothes,
washed themselves and cleaned themselves up.

How do they manage it if their whole surroundings are filthy?

They still get cleaned up. We can always show how, in
the midst of a dirty locality, our people's houses are clean.
And when the neighbours see, they notice a difference,
and they try to learn some of these things. We encourage
them to send their children to school, we encourage them
to stay clean.

When people stop drinking this makes a big difference –
more money is available and there are less problems in
the home.

What about sickness?

Sickness, real sickness, is much decreased. Primarily
because of hygiene. Secondly because they pray for their
problems, they don't go to the witch doctors any more.

Most of this teaching and change takes place from life to life,
as people meet in the cell groups:

As they come to the cell group meeting, there is a lot of
interaction so we don't really need to teach them, they will
see it and grasp it from each other. The general tendency
is that if you attend a new group where you are a stranger
you don't try to transform the group to your setting. You
transform yourself to fit into the group – that is the general
tendency. So when people come into cell groups they

don't really want to transform cell groups into their model but they tend to model themselves into the cell group settings. So that is something which happens naturally.

Reflection

Which approach is the most effective? Your answer is as good as mine. No one factor is enough to respond to the multiple causes of poverty and deprivation.

Change always begins with people, so working with individuals and community leaders is at the heart of any programme. But the factors that cause poverty are bigger than individuals, so harnessing government support and capital funding is also important.

Getting the balance right can be difficult: outside resources can encourage dependency. When fire and then flood devastated the slums on the bank of the Yamuna, people were forced out of their homes and on to the streets. Some of them are still there, because they find it easier to attract handouts.

For Gilbert the most important change is on the inside.

> We don't want to waste our energy or resources into just re-modelling and re-structuring their outside life. But we really want to see a change within themselves which will outburst in their life, in all the walks of their lives.

When this happens people become self-supporting rather than dependent. When they do receive gifts, for example clothes for distribution, they do their best to share them out as widely as possible. The cell group members decide who to give them to, rather than people from outside. This avoids dependency and encourages generosity.

Working with the urban poor clearly illustrates both the complex causes of the problems and the complex links between spiritual and socio-economic change.

Gilbert's church is in touch with about 3,500 people through 152 cell groups. Asha has seen change in about 20 slums. They both show what can be done, and there are other similar programmes. But there are more than 2,300 slum colonies in Delhi, with perhaps 8 million people (up from 6 million in 1992).

There's a long way to go; and time is running out.

10
Work, Worship and Witness:
Healing the Environment

More trees are being felled in India today at the hands of
dam, road and mine contractors than ever before... The
internal security of India in the next decade is more likely
to be threatened by water riots than wars or terrorism.
— *Bittu Sahgal*

The future must start with the small farmer and the
women. We must go back to the Gandhian concept of
production by the masses, though not of mass production.
— *M. S. Swaminathan*

I want to take Jesus' values and impact the real world with
them.
— *Ken Gnanakan*

Bangalore was India's fastest growing city in the 1970s.
In ten years it doubled in size, thanks to its excellent climate
and stable administration which attracted a proliferation of
industry – especially high-tech industries – businesses and
NGOs. It went on to become India's software capital (today
it competes with Hyderabad and Chennai).

It also became one of India's most polluted cities. In the

former Garden City traffic fumes choke the air, while the waste from crowded housing, factory effluents and plain lack of de-silting choke the waterways. Its many lakes are dying.

In late 1999 a group of CEOs from leading businesses, Corporation officials and Indian Air Force officers met community leaders of the villages around the Bellandur Lake, one of the largest. They agreed on a plan to reduce the pollution and restore the lake to its former state. Chairing the group was Ken Gnanakan, Director of ACTS Ministries. With his flowing white hair and *kurta pyjama*, Ken looks like a musician or poet, perhaps a painter. He is all three, as well as an academic and preacher. The long hair is probably the main link with Ken's past as lead guitarist and singer of the Trojans. Back in the 1960s they were a rock band that thrilled the hearts of clubbers in Calcutta, Bombay and Delhi.

I met Ken soon after arriving in Madras in 1966. It wasn't too long since he had undergone a life-changing experience. In Delhi he had met a group of young people who talked about Jesus' forgiveness and the power to overcome temptation. Ken decided to follow Jesus and experienced a deep change.

In Madras he had begun working with a youth organisation, using his skills in music and journalism. We had long talks about Indian society and bringing change. One of the favourite songs in the youth group we attended was:

> This land is your land, this land is my land,
> From the Himalayas down to Cape Comorin;
> From Bombay city to Old Calcutta
> This land was made for you and me.

The second verse began: 'This land needs Jesus, he is the answer.' We fervently believed the words but weren't altogether sure what they meant. We were still trying to identify the questions.

A few years later Ken and his wife Prema left for further studies in Australia and the UK. They returned in 1977 to set up the ACTS Institute in a couple of rented houses in south Bangalore. This was a project for a new kind of training for 'real people in the real world'. It would integrate daily work with worship and witness. So the trainees would learn a vocational skill (carpentry, metalwork, electronics, etc.) while also studying the Bible and preparing to preach. Ken's idea was that they would go all over India as a kind of 'barefoot preachers', supporting themselves with their work skills.

There were a lot of teething problems. Not everybody was comfortable with the combination of working with your hands to support yourself, while also preparing to be a 'holy man' or 'holy woman'. But the Institute grew. As it tried to serve the local community, it branched into health care and education, starting a clinic and school along with vocational training for disadvantaged people. Rural women learned tailoring alongside the ACTS graduates.

They were breaking new ground. But then two things happened which strongly influenced Ken's thinking and led him much further in new directions.

Encounter in the Village

The first was an experience: an encounter in one of the villages. The students used to visit the colonies and villages south of Bangalore to preach. They used music and dance to gather their audience and involve them in worship. Ken describes what happened on one occasion:

> The dance was delightful. The boys got into a circle and sang in Kannada. They soon moved into a rhythmic use of little sticks stepping out impressively to do the *kolattam*.
>
> Everyone gathered around happily, some even joining in

the dance. Having got their attention, the preacher began
the message.

Meanwhile, a man had been calmly watching all that was
going on. Losing no time now, he came into the empty
space inside the circle of people. Pulling away the
megaphone from the hand of the preacher he shouted,
'Stop this.' We were dumbfounded! Scared!

'This is a Western religion you are preaching. You are
wanting to make us Christians because of the money you
get,' he said.

The preacher having collected himself tried to say – 'Sir,
this is not a Western religion ... We are Indians ...'

'You may be Indians, but you are influenced by the West
and its money,' he reiterated.

We were all deeply disturbed.

The man had touched a nerve. Ken had been struggling with
these issues for some time. How could he be authentically
Indian? To what extent did the ACTS Institute, and the
church at large, reflect Indian culture? Like everybody else,
he was aware of many aspects that reflected outside cultural
elements – the architecture, the music, some styles of
worship. Some of it had been absorbed from the colonial
past. Some of it was current influence. The Coca-Cola culture
had its impact on Christians as much as on other Indians.
And then there was the popular image of the cinema:

I recalled the Christians depicted – the man, suited, with
a cigar in his mouth and a drink in his hand, a thief or a
pickpocket. The women – loudly dressed, the dancer, a
prostitute. Why, I asked, was this unfair association of the
West with Hollywood? And since Christianity came to us
from the West, was Hollywood culture to be our Christian
culture? The media seemed to play heavily on this fact,
determined to strengthen their claim that the West and
Christianity were synonymous.

Indian Culture?

The issue of Indian culture versus foreign influence is of course an endless debate and there are no easy answers. How do you decide? How far back do you go? Sunanda Datta-Ray, former editor of *The Statesman*, points out that it is 'impossible to say what is authentic in a culture that has survived unbroken for 5,000 years of migration, conquest, assimilation and evolution' (*The International Indian*, Millennium Issue).

A strict interpretation would forbid trousers and tea, cars, cycles and computers. But the traffic, these days, is in all directions. Indian restaurants (run by Bangladeshis) are by far the most popular in Britain. 'Chicken Tikka Masala' was recently declared Britain's national dish. In Birmingham they have combined it with another national dish to produce 'Chip-topped Chicken Curry'. The *tabla* and *sitar* are part of many bands. Yoga and ayurvedic medicine are prescribed around the world. You can get *puja* online from many temples, through the internet. The trend towards fusion, creating your own blend, seems to be universal. Sunanda Datta-Ray quotes Raj Kapoor's solution in the film *Shri 420*:

> *Mera joota hain Japani*
> *Yeh patloon Inglistani*
> *Sir pe lal topi Russi*
> *Phir bhi dil hai Hindustani*

(My shoes are Japanese, my trousers English, my red hat Russian – but my heart is Indian)

If the heart is Indian, does it matter about the outside...?

Of course it isn't that simple. Like an onion, culture has many layers, which you can't easily separate (peeling them may lead to tears). Nevertheless the outside does reflect what is inside, to an extent. So Ken struggled with this issue of

identity and culture. Even before the village incident, he had
made a personal change: he had given up his tie and jacket
and started wearing *kurta-pajama*.

But what about the church? Ken and his colleagues
worked hard to express their commitment to Christ in ways
that were authentically Indian – music (both folk and
classical), sitting on the floor, sharing food together. They
developed the idea of a 'church without walls' a building
with Indian architecture, open on all sides – *'Christalaya'*.
This was practical as well as symbolic. It meant that numbers
could contract or expand, while people could listen and
observe from the outside. They were always welcome to join
– or not – as they preferred.

Encounter with the Bible

The second influence came from Ken's own study of the
Bible. The more he read it the more he was drawn back to
its majestic opening words: 'In the beginning God created
the heavens and the earth'. It's a breathtaking, daring
perspective – one world, created by One God, good and
perfect. We didn't happen just by chance.

God the creator. As Ken reflected on this concept it
opened up 'a brand new world ... a common platform'. All
of us are created by the One God, sharing life on this one
planet. How do we express our humanness? How do we work
together to restore humanness, to restore our common world?

Back to the Environment

This took Ken back to his own roots in art and music. It
also led him to become involved in concern for the
environment. The right place to start was with educating the
children, which led to the formation of PEAS *(The
Programme for Environmental Awareness in Schools).*

PEAS was started in 1991. It began with visits to schools, talks, competitions and other events to attract their attention and get them involved. That led to the launch of a national magazine for children, and then to national conferences. The second conference, in November 1998, brought 700 children to Mumbai for four days which included visits from film stars and celebrities, educators and politicians:

> 'I am now learning from you', said former police chief Julio Ribeiro. 'My grandchildren are the ones who teach me about all that is happening to the environment.'

From PEAS it was natural for Ken to get involved in other environmental projects, especially waste disposal and the conservation of water. One thing led to another and eventually to the challenge of the Bellandur Lake.

To make things happen requires action and the right skills. They recruited an environment engineer from Germany, an expert in waste control; Ecki is co-ordinating the project to clean up the lake.

Ken is a consultant to the Indira Gandhi National Open University (IGNOU) on environmental issues, and has written a distance-learning course for the university.

India's eco-warriors

The environmental movement is one of the most significant developments over the last twenty years in India.

The Chipko movement in the Himalayan foothills was one of the first to attract wide attention. Women tied themselves to trees to prevent the commercial logging that was destroying the forests. The leader of the movement, Sunderlal Bahuguna, drew inspiration from an earlier generation of women in Rajasthan who had done the same to protect trees in 1730. (Paradoxically, in the same region fuel-starved villagers still cut off branches and leaves to burn, destroying many trees in the process).

The protest against the Narmada Dam has become an international cause, due to the bravery and determination of leaders like Medha Patkar and more recently the intervention of the writer Arundhati Roy.

Indian farmers have shown great powers of organisation and self-discipline, not just to demonstrate for their own interests (e.g. against the export of onions) but also to take on the might of the genetically modified (GM) food corporations. They argue that the introduction of GM seeds could lead to a kind of neo-colonialism, in which India's farmers become dependent on the huge multi-national seed and fertiliser giants. GM crops could threaten bio-diversity and benefit only the rich, squeezing out the small farmers, who are already under pressure. The results would be disastrous for all.

There are alternatives. Vandana Shiva, a leading environmental activist, points to projects where women have learned to combine traditional agricultural ways with new environmental insights. Working on a small scale, they have doubled their output and become self-reliant, even in poor quality land.

Indian farmers have been around the world with their message, targeting groups like the G8 Summit in Cologne in 1999. They have campaigned not only on the GM issue but the whole process of globalisation.

On a much smaller scale, people all over India, urban and rural, are becoming aware that these are important issues and that each of us is responsible to play our part. It need not mean campaigning or high-profile activities. It could be simply working locally to dispose our waste more effectively, as well as considering how we could waste less.

It could be finding a way to benefit others through your business, as well as using resources better. Nitin and Antara

Dave are a young couple in Bangalore. Antara, a passionate animal lover, works for a charitable organisation involved in education and training with rural women. Nitin works for a multi-national freight and courier company. For the last two years the company's annual greeting card has been designed by children at the local branch of the Society for children with cerebral palsy, where Nitin helps as a volunteer. The children love it and the cards are innovative and attractive.

Inter-connected

The more you get into it the more you realise that every aspect leads to another. They are all inter-connected – economic and political, social and cultural, ethical and spiritual.

Where do you begin? Ken Gnanakan's starting point is the fact that this is God's world – the title of a book he wrote on the environment was simply that: 'God's World'. God made the world and us, and we are part of his amazing creation. So we need to respect what God has made, to be good stewards, caring for it, discovering its unending potential, exploring its resources and using them for the good of all.

> As I realised that this is God's creation, I felt a compulsion to get in and get involved, to engage with the needs.

The more we discover of God's creation, the more we respect it. For example, the tulsi plant is amazing because it has so many uses. Or the coconut, the groundnut, rubber and so many other parts of God's creation.

But what about the problems? How do you deal with pollution? Pollution has many causes, some due to economic factors, some based on ignorance. So education and the right resources are essential. But many aspects of the problem originate in human greed and selfishness, the desire for quick profit - and corruption.

In a hard-hitting and exhaustive analysis, S. S. Gill, a former high-ranking civil servant, describes corruption as a cancer at the heart of India. (S. S. Gill, *The Pathology of Corruption*, 1998). Among many factors he analyses the place of wealth, sin and power in the world-view of an Indian. These moral, cultural and social factors, in some cases deep in our sub-conscious memory, profoundly affect the way we think and act.

Ken Gnanakan takes seriously the Bible's teaching on human sin and the fall. He would agree with S. S. Gill that 'the idea of sin burns like a carbuncle' at the heart of the Bible's teaching. God made the world good; human beings have spoiled it through our rebellion against God and our turning to our selfish ways.

How does that affect our approach to environmental issues? Some might argue that we should keep ourselves pure by concentrating on 'spiritual' matters, rather than run the risk of getting our hands dirty. But for Ken, Jesus is his model:

> Jesus was very involved in his situation, addressing real issues, politically, socially, culturally. I want to take Jesus' values and impact the real world with them. In my environmental work, it is his values that we take there. Jesus addressed his context. He was truly human, relating to every aspect of life and meeting needs as he encountered them.
>
> Salvation enables us to become human. Being in Christ makes us fully human, more able to appreciate the hurt and damage, the aches and pains of the world, and be able to be restorers in that situation.

When you get involved in communities, one change leads to another. For example, when the Aroles at Jamkhed showed people that the way to better health was through better hygiene and digging drains, the people soon realised that it wasn't enough to dig a drain from their own home. Their neighbour needed to do the same, otherwise the flies and the dirt would still be there. So they needed to work together, as a community and not just as individuals. When the children were fed, they all had to contribute to the common meal. But then they found that it wasn't always easy to work together. There might be caste barriers, or one family might have a grudge against the other. Jealousy or resentment could easily come in. That led them to realise the need for forgiveness and acceptance.

Reflection

Changing your environment is not just a matter of digging drains or having enough money for new projects (though it does mean that). It goes deeper and affects the social, the moral and the spiritual.

Here again, Ken sees Jesus as the model. Jesus mixed with all kinds of people, religious and secular, the respectable and the marginalised. He was at home with working men, religious teachers, women of doubtful character, corrupt officials. He broke boundaries and accepted people just as they were. He didn't condemn their sin, but he offered them forgiveness and acceptance. The word that best sums this up is *krupa* ('grace') – his unjudging friendship to all, whether they deserved it or not:

> To be able to get down and mingle with the poor, that takes a certain amount of grace. That knocks down your pride. Grace is the catalyst that brings about these little changes. To be able to go and live amidst sin and sinful people and not to be judging them ... not to assimilate nor condemn, but to be an agent of change.
> Without grace, we find it very hard to intervene in this world.

11

In Two Worlds: The Contribution
of the Diaspora

The Contribution of the Diaspora

India's key Independence leaders were almost all NRIs.
— *Sam Pitroda*

Some Indian success gene ensures that Indians appear in rich lists and success stories across the globe.
— *Ram Gidoomal*

The decisive ideas that have made India would all be ideas that have allowed Indians to make themselves.
— *Sunil Khilnani*

The 'idea of India' is rapidly expanding. As the country's population passes the billion mark, exports continue to grow – not just pickles and carpets but people, with brains and talent, imagination and ability. Nearly 20 million Non-Resident Indians (NRIs) live and work outside the subcontinent, from Hong Kong to Los Angeles, Nairobi to Philadelphia, Sydney to Trinidad, Jakarta to Hamburg, Manila to London. Not all of them appear in the rich lists and success stories. Many have struggled to survive. Many never planned to stay away from 'home'; they believed in the 'myth of return' but their children don't.

NRIs come in all shapes and sizes. One thing they all have in common is that they belong to more than one culture. They have learnt how to adapt, how to benefit from their new environment, as well as to make a contribution. They have a choice, as the culture keeps changing, both 'back home' and in the new culture where the next generation is growing up. They can remain stuck in some ideal culture of the past, or they can keep on changing.

The Diaspora is the place where I have personally found my own identity as someone who belongs to more than one culture, who can be at home in both and perhaps a bridge between them. Some NRIs have found that they can cross the divisions that have plagued South Asia. There is more that unites them with their neighbours from Pakistan or Bangladesh or Sri Lanka, than divides them.

Being away from India brings up new perspectives and the space for reflection. It's an opportunity to bring change and make a contribution; not just of money, and not just in one direction.

London Links

London is in many ways the Diaspora's hub, with nearly 2 million Asians in the UK and with its intersecting economic, political and social links.

I first met **Ram Gidoomal** in London in 1988. He was a businessman who had been expelled with his family from Kenya in the late1960s. They arrived almost penniless in the UK and started off in a corner shop in Shepherds Bush, West London. At the time we met, Ram had just returned from a visit to Bombay which had had a profound impact on him. Shoko and I had also just arrived back from India and were looking for the next step while our children finished school and started university. We were introduced by a mutual friend, **Dr Raju Abraham**, a consultant neurophysiologist with the NHS. Raju's family were from Kerala but he was born and brought up in Maharashtra. He had trained as a doctor at Vellore and travelled and worked in several countries before settling in London. Raju and Ram had been meeting regularly for some months, along with **Prabhu Guptara**, a management consultant originally from Delhi, now based in Switzerland. As we talked, shared ideas and prayed, we struck up an unlikely partnership that has continued in its freewheeling way and grown considerably.

Our interest was the South Asian community, both in South Asia and scattered around the world. How could we use this network creatively to serve people of all communities without distinction? How could the resources of the Diaspora flow back to South Asia?

The first project was *Christmas Cracker*, dreamed up along with Steve Chalke, a well-known youth leader whose father was Indian. Christmas Cracker encouraged young people to set up 'Eat Less, Pay More' restaurants during the Christmas period. They would charge outrageous prices for simple food, or a glass of water, and use all the profits for charity. Christmas Cracker was launched in 1989 and proved a great success. Its secret was in giving young people responsibility, training them to take practical action and to develop new skills, for example running restaurants or, in later Cracker projects, operating radio stations and editing special local newspapers.

Soon afterwards *South Asian Concern* was started as a registered charity, specifically to serve the Asian community through different avenues – business, development, health – and to help develop leadership among Asians.

We quickly ran into a fascinating question.

Ram was being interviewed on TV Asia.

'Why is Jesus always shown with blue eyes and blond hair?' the interviewer asked.

'That is because the church has become very European in its outlook,' Ram replied. 'Jesus actually came from the Middle East. He wore sandals and walked along dusty roads, just like the people of South Asia.'

We realised we had to learn how to show the relevance of Christ within Asian culture. Ram began to write *Sari 'n' Chips*, a book describing his own experiences of adjusting to life in the UK. It was an immediate bestseller. All over Britain people wrote or phoned to say 'You described my situation exactly. I never knew that others had experienced the same issues.'

The book was followed by two albums of 'fusion music', *Songs of the Kingdom* and *Asia Worships*. They combined Asian and Western music, with songs in Hindi, Urdu, English, Gujarati and Malayalam. They were immensely popular, bridging the gap both for non-Asians looking for multi-cultural music and for young British Asians living in two worlds – the world of their parents 'back home', and the world in which they were growing up at school and college.

Ram himself had undergone profound change as a student.

My family had been twice forced into homelessness and migration – first from newly-created Pakistan in 1947, then from newly-independent East Africa where we had lived in palatial splendour and controlled huge financial interests. Now we were refugees in Shepherds Bush, West London. We had just enough money to buy a corner shop, with a flat above it where sixteen of us lived. We prospered and were eventually running a chain of shops in West London.

The work ethic directed our lives. I chose to read physics at Imperial College in London. It was during my final year as an undergraduate, when I had to stay on site at the campus, that I realised how difficult it was to live away from the security of the extended family. I was attempting to drown my sorrows in the pub when I heard a group of rock musicians called 'The Forerunners' playing in the background. They interspersed their music with stories of how each of them had met Jesus, and how their lives had been transformed as a result. I was intrigued. They talked about a God who loved the world so much that he sent his one and only son as a once and for all sacrifice for sin.

Sin for me was my karmic debt: the difference between my bad *karma* and my good *karma*, not only from this life but from my previous incarnations. The principle of *karma*, 'what you sow you reap', was a fundamental part of my Hindu and Sikh upbringing. And sitting in the pub that evening I realised that Jesus was offering a way out of my karmic debt. By my own reckoning I was spiritually bankrupt. My bad *karma* far outweighed any good that I had done.

I decided to conduct my own research around the claims of Jesus. As I studied the events, people and places recorded in the Bible, I found my prejudices against Christ being exposed. For a start, Jesus was a Middle Easterner, not a white man with blue eyes and blond hair.

All the discoveries I made about Christianity were exciting and helpful, but how could I accept Jesus as my Saviour and the Bible as my point of reference? That would be a step of faith. I would be surrendering my life into the hands of Jesus and submitting myself to his sovereignty. Not an easy decision for a scientist and a self-made businessman.

One evening, as I read the Book of Revelation, I came across the words of Jesus: 'Behold, I stand at the door and knock: if anyone hears my voice and opens the door, I will come in to him and will eat with him and he with me.' Knowing the importance to our culture of eating together, these words made a profound impression on me. I was being offered the fellowship and friendship that I was desperately seeking. I got down on my knees and prayed a simple prayer, accepting Jesus into my life.

I was taking the radical step of following Jesus Christ. Now I had found what religion had told me was worth seeking above all: a *Sanatana Sat Guru*, an eternal, true Guru, a living and personal way.

I struggled, from the outset, to relate my new-found faith – constantly being explained to me from a Western perspective – to my Eastern upbringing. I had to show my extended family and community that following Jesus was not just a white, colonial, imperialistic option.

Pursuing that struggle led Ram back into the world of business consultancy, helping to interpret the Asian community to the mainstream, and then into politics. He gained 100,000 votes in the London Mayoral election in May 2000.

Health Transformation?

In 1991 Raju Abraham returned to India with his family. He began by taking a sabbatical, but eventually resigned from the NHS to concentrate his efforts in India. He worked as a consultant for Emmanuel Hospital Association, a growing health care programme with hospitals and community health projects all across North India. EHA was providing quality health care but Raju challenged the leaders to move beyond physical healing to the inner, spiritual change that is also important for people's health. EHA now sees itself as a

'Fellowship for Transformation'. It aims to serve people in every dimension of life, working with the community and meeting felt needs.

Vinod Shah, EHA's Director, explains their philosophy:

> We serve people and care for them because Christ did. God made us whole people. He made the body and when something goes wrong with it we have a responsibility to respond. We have to show love, whether people respond to that love or not. It is Christ-like to address the problem of suffering. We also take appropriate opportunities to talk about our faith. It isn't because we want to convert someone, or change his attitudes. If you make a link like that, it will affect your care, if that person doesn't do what you expect him to do.

But why care for the poor? Are they more gullible, more vulnerable?

> We care for the poor because Jesus had that bias. It was not a prejudice; it was a bias to restore the balance, because socio-economic and cultural factors gave a favourable balance to a particular section of society, while the others missed out. We provide a support to them. But we don't agree that they are more gullible or we can influence them more easily.
>
> There are literally hundreds of ways of serving a community. The basic thing is to identify with the community, to win their confidence, to really love. It's not a trick to show them that you love them. It's actually to love them.

Vinod Shah's own experience underlies his views. He comes from a Jain business family, originally from Porbander in Gujarat, where Mahatma Gandhi was born.

> We come from the same caste (and sub-caste) as Mahatma Gandhi, so we were very proud of him. We had his books, we read about him a lot. He was our Bible in matters of conduct. One of the things that I read was his

recommendation that we should read Jesus' Sermon on the Mount. So when I went to Madras to study at Loyola College, I asked for a copy of the Sermon on the Mount and I was given the New Testament. I remember reading it and being immediately captivated by the person of Christ. About five years later I decided to follow Christ.

Other creative avenues opened up for EHA through Raju Abraham's link with the Diaspora. In 1993 a massive earthquake devastated two districts of Maharashtra. Ram Gidoomal and Steve Chalke approached GMTV, a popular breakfast TV channel in Britain, who agreed to launch an appeal. Aided by 'Mr Motivator', GMTV's celebrity fitness expert, they raised over £40,000 to build a new hospital and community health programme in the devastated area. The 'GMTV Priya Hospital' was opened at Dapegaon in 1995, named after Priya, a little girl who was found unhurt in the earthquake ruins.

In 1999 the Kosovo crisis filled TV screens with pictures of exhausted refugees. An Asian businessman approached Ram Gidoomal with the offer of money to send medical help to Kosovo. 'What if we could organise a team from India?' asked Ram.

'I would give you double the money!' replied the delighted businessman.

EHA was able to send two teams to work with the refugees in Albania. Paul East, Director of EHA (UK), co-ordinated the operation from the European end. The logistics were formidable, including getting the visas, organising transit through Greece or Italy, and negotiating disturbed areas.

The EHA doctors made a great contribution and also learned a lot themselves. Three months later, when the cyclone struck Orissa in October 1999, it was natural for

EHA to send the same teams to contribute to the relief and development effort. They were able to respond in a similar way to the Gujarat earthquake of January 2001.

Changing India

In the last fifteen years the pace of change has been intense in India and the Diaspora. When Rajiv Gandhi took over after his mother's death in 1984, few knew whether he would survive politically, or could bring any real change. A technocrat rather than a politician, he put his faith in computers and education. In a remarkable speech at the Congress Centenary Celebrations in Mumbai, he described his vision of India's transformation, through education.

Rajiv did not live to see his dreams fulfilled, but the liberalisation of the Indian economy from 1991 was the continuation of policies he initiated. And the phenomenal success of India's software industry bears out his faith in the power of the computer.

Communications Revolution

One of the most fascinating transformations in India in the 1990s was due to an NRI. Until then telephoning in India had always been an exercise in frustration. Trying to make a long-distance call was like a game of roulette. You never knew if you could succeed. The 'engaged' tone was the most familiar sound – and it didn't mean that the other person was 'on the phone. It just meant that you couldn't get through. You kept on dialling, trying different techniques of twirling the dial (quickly, slowly, using a different rhythm …) hoping and praying that you might connect. When you did get through, it was touch and go how long you would stay connected. And you often had to shout to be heard. Sharad Borde, one of our colleagues in Pune, was famous for his telephone manner.

You could hear him from the other end of the college building. Whether the person at the other end of the phone could hear him was another matter.

By the early 1990s, all that had begun to change. Telephone booths sprang up at every corner, offering STD (long distance) and ISD (international) calls. You got through the first time and you didn't need to shout. Your time and cost were clearly shown on the LCD display and when you had finished you simply paid. Today you can phone anywhere in India, or around the world.

What made the difference? The secret is a man called **Sam Pitroda**, an NRI who went to America and invented a number of electronic devices, including an electronic switch that eliminated the need for moving parts in a telephone exchange – the cause of major problems in India, where heat and dust play havoc with the connections. Sam Pitroda wanted to do something for India and he felt he could contribute through radical change in telecommunications. So he came back and tried to meet Indira Gandhi to share his vision. The first time he was told he would have to wait at least a year to meet her. He came back a year later, and again, until finally he was given an interview and was then allowed to set up a new corporation to devise the technology. The results came in just a few years.

The revolution continues, not always smoothly. Mobile phones and Internet cafes are the current flag-bearers. Attempts to decentralise the telecommunications industry keep running into opposition from vested interests. The software and the whiz-kids aren't always a match for the bureaucratic mindset and the fortress mentality.

In 1993 Shoko and I heard about e-mail for the first time in Delhi. We decided to get connected. I heard that e-mail was already available in India: the place to go was the Videsh

Sanchar Nigam head office, near Connaught Place. I arrived outside the tall, imposing building and attempted to walk through the gate. I was immediately stopped by the sentry and the gate was closed.

'I want to enquire about your e-mail facilities', I explained to the sentry. He shook his head. It was impossible to go in. After further discussion he pointed me to a booth on the other side of the gate, where another sentry was sitting. There was a telephone in the booth, and I was allowed to phone one of the officials inside. A scientist answered and I explained my interest. He took my address and promised to send a leaflet by post. It duly arrived and answered all the technical questions with great clarity. But the process of actually applying for the facility was fearsome – almost as difficult as getting a new phone connection. We gave up the idea and subscribed to Compuserve instead.

But compare the telephones with those of twenty years ago: there is no comparison!

Reflection

Needed: Champions

Back in London Ram Gidoomal organised a lecture to be given in January 1999 by Sam Pitroda at the House of Lords. In the lecture, Sam reflected on his vision for India. He saw technology as a means of radical transformation, just as his intervention had sparked off the telecommunications revolution. But technology alone was not enough. It needed a different mindset and 'champions' to push it through.

The Internet revolution could have been developed by India because it has the brain power. Every week five Indian kids become millionaires through the Internet in California. We need to tap this talent from outside the country. Our problem is the inability to implement ... We know what to do but don't do it. We need champions for each of the major causes that the country faces – water, sanitation, literacy, teamwork, management skills, vision ... We need to develop a minimum critical mass. Then we will be able to network large numbers of people.

He identified ten major areas where change was needed and called for 'champions' for each one – people who would be honest, transparent, committed team players, willing to give rather than to receive. Sam reminded his audience that the majority of India's independence leaders had been NRIs. His challenge was to harness NRI resources and creativity once again, for the benefit of India, and ultimately the world.

Responsible Citizenship

Malini Mehra seems to be the kind of person he was looking for. An activist and campaigner on human rights and environmental issues, who has lived and worked in several countries, she started the Centre for Social Markets (CSM) in 2000 to face the challenge of corporate citizenship: 'It is no longer enough to simply make a profit and pay taxes. Businesses are now expected to act responsibly, be accountable and benefit society as a whole.'

Malini Mehra believes that British Asians can take a lead in this, with their strong traditions of hard work and responsibility to family and community. An Indian citizen, she currently travels between offices in London and Calcutta. CSM's goal is 'to change the way markets work for the public and environmental good by changing the behaviour of market actors', through education, research and advocacy. It has a particular focus on Diaspora communities such as South Asians and Chinese, to exert positive pressure for change 'back home', as well as where they are placed. CSM believes all businesses should be enterprising, for the 'triple bottom line' of 'people, planet and profit'. It holds conferences on topics like sustainability and transparency.

Changing behaviour... exerting positive pressure for change ... That's what all of us would like to be doing. The Diaspora clearly has a key role in catalysing change. But what do we really mean by change in people? And how do we hope to bring it in India?

12
Change is Inevitable:
But What Is It?

Hindu civilisation's ... gift to mankind, the extraordinary
and possibly singular ability to absorb, to assimilate, and,
in the process, be enriched by human diversity.
— *Vinod Mehta*

Other nations move forward through progress of some
kind or the other. India moves forward, paradoxical!y, by
remembering her old self.
— *Deepak Chopra*

India's greatest ability is its capacity to absorb change, says
Vinod Mehta, editor of *Outlook* magazine:

Among the handful of ideas which have nurtured and
sustained India these past one thousand years, one
according to me is central: the spirit of benign tolerance.
Our sometimes wobbly republic must never forget to build
and consolidate and celebrate Hindu civilisation's
timeless, perhaps unique, gift to mankind, the
extraordinary and possibly singular ability to absorb, to
assimilate, and, in the process, be enriched by human
diversity ...

Our foreign friends ascribe the resilience to 'fatalism and

its attendant benefits'. But that is too facile an explanation for an infinitely more complex civilisational habit.'

(*Outlook*, 15 November 1999)

Over the last millennium India has absorbed change from all directions – Turkish, Mongol, Persian, European, American, Japanese, global. In the last fifty years the pace of change has accelerated almost beyond recognition. Independence brought a flowering of activity and expectations – political, spiritual, social, scientific and industrial. Not all the aspirations were met. The Green Revolution of the 1970s brought a new freedom from hunger. The closing years of the century saw a burst of technical and economic change. The communications revolution and the global economy, for all the dangers they bring, have also brought India and her people into the mainstream of change in a way they have not been since the 1950s.

But in this process, what has really changed? Is the ability to absorb and assimilate a virtue, a 'gift to mankind'? Of course it is, in one sense. But could it also be a way of avoiding the need to make choices? Are all changes equally desirable? Or, to put it another way, if we accept certain changes will it mean the rejection of existing attitudes or practices?

Can we assimilate without critical assessment and choice?

What is Change and Where Does it Come From?

1. Change comes from all directions

Travelling by train in India is part of a continuous social revolution. When the railways began in the 1850s some people saw them as symbols of enslavement and pollution. As the steel lines began to cross the country, along with the telegraph wires, they compared them to steel bands slowly throttling and defiling the land. Today Indian Railways covers 60,000 kilometres and carries 4 billion passengers every year: four journeys for every Indian.

When you travel by train you mix with people of every background. It is true that there are different classes of travel, but they are based on what you can afford, rather than which community you were born into. And they keep changing. In 1970 Third-Class rail travel was abolished at a stroke. It was an egalitarian gesture. What they actually did was to remove the old Second Class carriages and then paint out the third stroke of the III on the Third-Class compartments. Some painting contractors made their fortunes that year. Today there are at least seven classes of travel to choose from.

Once you get into your compartment, whichever class, you mix with people from all over India. The first time I travelled on the old GT Express, heading northward from Madras, I was struck to see North Indian faces and hear Hindi spoken again, which I hadn't heard since my childhood. In the sleeper compartments (Third-Class or Second-Class, 3 Tier or 2 Tier) you are together with your fellow travellers for a day or night, or even longer. You talk, swap stories, play cards, make friends, exchange ideas and addresses. In the unreserved compartments you fight ferociously to get on. Some pay a coolie to get them a seat or, better still, a luggage rack on which to stretch out for the night. But once everybody is in, you settle down and join together to keep others out at the next station.

Eating is one of the great pleasures and preoccupations of a long train journey. And watching what others eat is part of the enjoyment. In the really old days, when we were children, Spencers used to do the catering on the Southern Railway. You ordered a meal, or tea and toast, at one station.

A telegraph message ensured that it would be delivered to
you at the next by a turbaned waiter in a white uniform.
Those days went long ago. Today the main opportunity
for eating comes at a station, where the passengers fan out
in search of their chosen favourite – *aloo puri, dosai,*
omelette and bread, *jellabis,* bananas or oranges. At one time
they introduced a dining car on some trains, which you had
to enter at one station and leave at another. Nowadays every
long-distance train has its own pantry car and a continuous
stream of tea, coffee, snacks and meals. Or you travel by
Shatabdi Express and your food is part of the ticket, as it is
when you fly. Of course, the more conservative or fastidious
passengers always bring their own food. They wouldn't risk
pollution or indigestion from eating something cooked
outside their own kitchen.

The concept of a timetable is something introduced by
the railways. It's still a relative concept. On a journey of
twenty-four hours, what difference does half an hour make
– or even two or three? Shoko returned from a visit to Japan,
where trains are scheduled to the nearest second (and they
do leave and arrive with frightening accuracy). Her train from
Delhi to Pune arrived eight hours late and nobody appeared
to be concerned. She found it strangely relaxing. Off the main
line, travelling by passenger train, time returns to the village
concept of days measured by the sun, rather than hours or
minutes.

For all their comforting sameness and lateness, the
railways have actually been at the forefront of introducing
new technology. In the old days of steam you would arrive
black and sooty from your journey. Today the trains are diesel
or electric, air-conditioned, fast and super-fast. The railways
made extensive use of the telegraph. They had their own
telephone system and then microwave communication. They

invested heavily in electronic signalling and later in computerised reservation systems. At Chennai Central the Arrivals and Departures appear on a huge digital screen, interspersed with full-colour advertisements.

The railways have enabled people of every class to travel all over India and see people and places completely outside their own domestic world. Millions travel each day to work, some commuting for three hours each way. The railways enable mass movements and political demonstrations. They truly belong to the people of India.

Multiple Sources of Change

The railways are just one example of the multiple sources of change in India. Education, literacy, factories and dams, films and books – each could tell its own story of the way it has shaped and changed our lives.

Some changes were intentional. The government has been a major source of planned change through legislation, such as the positive discrimination of the Reservation policies enshrined in the Constitution. Some would argue that there has been too much change, for too few. But the changes have been profound nevertheless. The upstairs restaurant at Chennai Central has been there as long as I can remember, though its menus have changed over the years. On a recent visit the waiter told me he had worked there for thirty-six years. For the first fifteen he was paid only on a commission basis. In 1978 new laws meant that his job became permanent and he received fixed wages.

Other changes seem just to have happened. When Shoko and I returned to India in 1991, after just three years away, we were immediately assaulted by evidence of the satellite and TV revolution that was taking place. An enormous satellite dish on a neighbour's roof fed a variety of channels to all the houses in the street. Instead of the highly regulated Doordarshan channel, viewers suddenly had a choice of half a dozen channels. They could get up-to-the-minute news from CNN or BBC, watch Michael Fish forecasting the weather over China, Madonna gyrating on MTV, or Amitabh Bachhan on a golden oldie film channel. Suddenly the world was on India's doorstep, for better or for worse. Coinciding with economic liberalisation, it meant that a whole range of goods were available. The old distinctions between Indian and foreign goods, often with dramatic differences in price and quality, began to disappear.

The more recent software and IT revolutions have not only changed the way that information is available. They have also created a new group of small businesses, started by people who are not from the usual business community. Today's computer science graduate would have studied engineering a few years ago and gone to work as a salaried employee. Instead he is now able to set up his own company, creating software or providing consultancy, working from his own home with a minimum of staff. A whole new class of entrepreneurs and even millionaires has been created in India, not to mention the Indian dotcom millionaires of Silicon Valley.

2. *Change is complex*

Professor Amartya Sen has often analysed what we mean by words like 'development', 'progress' and 'economic change'. If we want to measure real change in any society, we need to use a wide range of indicators, both positive and negative. Most people put *economic* reform and progress at the top of their list. But along with that there must be *access* to the opportunities it brings, so that many can benefit, not just the privileged few. That will require increased *literacy*, *basic health care, micro-credit schemes* and *land reform*. We will also need a reduction in *infant and maternal mortality, social exclusion* and *gender inequalities*. All of these factors need to be included in assessing change.

Professor Sen, an atheist, was accused of being a Christian missionary because he advocated much wider provision of elementary schooling, along the lines of the Chinese model. Compared to China, India has many more university graduates and higher education, but a lower proportion of elementary education. China has attempted economic reform without political change (while the former Soviet Union fell into near-chaos through an over-hasty and perhaps forced attempt to do both). India has chosen to work on different fronts – a planned economy *and* multi-party democracy – at different times, with different speeds: sometimes dramatically fast, other times painfully slow.

India is already diverse – there are great differences between local, regional, national cultures. The gap between city and village is enormous. In 1987 I went with a group of students from Pune to stay in a village just 200 kilometres away. It was the first time in their lives that they had been without electricity and running water. And the early morning experience of the 'field' toilets was traumatic.

Single changes don't always have the expected result. In Chennai the Slum Clearance Board put up apartment blocks for people living in huts. They moved in, then quickly found tenants to live there and pay them rent while they moved back to their old huts. The change of environment apparently wasn't attractive enough for them to change their lifestyle. Or maybe they were just smarter and more willing to make sacrifices than anybody realised.

A sadder example is the Todas, one of the ancient tribes of the Nilgiris, in South India. As school children we used to visit their huts above the Botanical Gardens. They were barrel-shaped, with a tiny entrance. Inside they were smoky, with no light or ventilation. The well-meaning government re-housed them in new concrete buildings, with good-sized doors and windows, plenty of light and ventilation. But the Todas were not prepared; they caught colds and pneumonia and some died. They needed other ways to help them adjust to change – better health care, information about nutrition, ways of heating their draughty new homes.

That has been the big lesson of community health and community development – you need to respond to multiple needs, because they are all inter-connected.

3. *Change comes from inside*

Long-term changes are happening all around us, from the sort of external sources we have just been describing. We have to accept them – not uncritically – and try to adjust. Kofi Annan, the UN Secretary General, tells us that globalisation is a fact of life, which demands that we find new moral solutions.

These changes are important. But they are not usually the source of transformation in a community or individuals. Deep change begins in the mind and heart.

This has been the most striking lesson from all the stories in this book. In Jamkhed, the transformation of the community's health began when thinking and attitudes were changed. In the tribal forests of Orissa, the villages of Andhra Pradesh, the slums of Delhi, the hills of the North East, or the comfortable suburbs of Chennai, Bangalore and London, people's lives were changed from the inside, when they were challenged or inspired to change their thinking and values. Instead of just accepting passively what was happening around them – good or bad – they became agents of change themselves.

These changes in values and attitudes combined to bring a change in their behaviour. As a result, the environment of their community changed.

Each of the friends whose stories I have told has experienced profound inner change, which motivated them to bring change to others. They joined thousands of others, from the social reformers of the nineteenth and twentieth centuries (and long before that) down to the present, who were determined to *do* something about the needs they saw around them.

4. Change can bring conflict

Change can be both good and bad and can often bring tension. The TV revolution brought up-to-date news and awareness of current events. It also brought the worst aspects of global culture – sex, violence, and unbridled materialism – which parents and traditionalists found impossible to counter.

When the tribal societies of North East or Central India encountered the modern world all of a sudden, they found it hard to keep the old and new together. The old traditions were usually the ones that went, to be replaced by the less attractive aspects of modern society – drink, drugs and unemployment.

Change also brings conflict when it challenges the status quo. The awakening consciousness of Dalits and OBCs ('Other Backward Communities') in Bihar challenges the feudal society. Environmental protesters oppose the vested interests of big business or the blind belief in technology of bureaucrats in New Delhi or state capitals.

Some of those who want to bring change actually initiate violence themselves, like the private armies in Bihar. Naxalites, Maoists, and any number of pressure groups for regional autonomy, have resorted to violence. Some did it willingly, others were forced into it. This moral dilemma between ends and means is not new. Freedom fighters in the independence struggle agonised over the issue of violence, with Gandhiji continually urging non-violence as the ideal.

Christians have struggled over this issue. Some who have espoused theologies of liberation for the masses, the Dalits or women, have argued that it may be necessary to use violence to bring about change. Others have argued that in the Bible change is not by people taking violence into their own hands. Power does not flow from the barrel of a gun, nor even from 'the people'. It comes from God and he brings change, by changing people's motivation and priorities, rather than one class or community replacing another.

Those who talk about India's gift for assimilation and absorption sometimes appear to imply that this is effortless. But deep changes don't take place without effort and sometimes struggle. When they do appear to have been effortless, it probably means that one group has dominated another and taken it over.

5. Change is inevitable

India is changing, all the time, from all directions and from multiple, sometimes conflicting, sources. Change is inevitable. And we all have a part in it. We all experience change and we can all try to resist it or to help bring it about.

What Are the Options in Facing Change?

We have basically three choices in responding to change. T. K Oommen of Jawaharlal Nehru University summarises them like this:

- **Isolation or Withdrawal** : Some of us don't want to change at all: we would like to stick to our traditions, maintain the status quo, keep our conservative attitudes.

- **Assimilation :** Some tell us that we should accept all changes as equally valid. Our society is very diverse and each group has something to give. No way of life is better or worse. So let us absorb changes as they come, from whatever direction, as gracefully as we can.

- **Selective Accommodation :** Change selectively and critically, say some. Take certain aspects of change that are offered, but not others. For example, make use of western technology, but don't follow western attitudes like unbridled individualism, rejection of old people, or worship of young people.

Each has its advantages and disadvantages.

Isolation is what some people appear to want for others, like the tribals. Of course it means withdrawal, giving up the struggle.

Assimilation looks attractive. Clearly we need to accept and respect the contribution of all the different groups in our society and outside. In practice this approach means following the majority. It often means being assimilated or absorbed ourselves. Real diversity is hard to maintain on this view. For centuries India has handled diversity by *encapsulating* the different groups, assigning them to a particular place in society, from which they cannot move. This (the caste system) has been its way of absorbing different social groups, and enabling them to live together in harmony. But it works best for you if you belong to a privileged part of the system.

Selective accommodation seems to offer a positive way forward. But like everything, it has its price. Selection can work well in some areas, for example wearing certain clothes or adopting technology. The Japanese excel at changing their appearance in the external world (high-tech, Western fashions) while apparently keeping their internal values at home (kimonos, Eastern calm).

But external and internal aspects of a culture are in fact linked to each other, some more obviously than others. So it isn't always easy to control the results of the changes we accept, as we have seen with the TV and Internet revolutions. And change in some areas results in rejection of others. This can lead to conflict, as we have seen repeatedly.

But the biggest question that this approach raises is: How do we decide which aspects of change are good? How do we choose? What values do we follow? Who chooses?

13

Conversion: What Kind of Change Does It Bring?

> Conversions occur when people have no idea of themselves, and have no means of understanding or retrieving their past.
>
> — *V.S. Naipaul*

> Religion has caused enough conflict in India. Are you trying to add one more?
>
> — *An Australian tourist*

India is changing. And we all have a part in it, for better or worse. How do we decide the way our lives, or our society, should change? What are the criteria to determine where we should go?

And how do we know when we have got there? What is the point at which an individual or a community has been 'transformed'? When does 'real change' take place?

Everybody will answer differently, of course. Amartya Sen has already cautioned us against any narrow description. Addressing the 1999 World Health Assembly, he regarded the 'freedom to live long and to live well' as very important ingredients. The word 'freedom' itself, in that context, implies a number of other key factors.

The World Health Organisation's own definition of health describes it as a state of 'physical, mental, social and spiritual well-being, and not just the absence of disease'.

The spiritual dimension is often the last to be included but is actually basic to any meaningful state of well-being. Nobody in India would disagree. India surely has enough spirituality of her own, enough to share with the whole world? The questions only come when we seek to define 'spirituality' or compare alternatives. That has led to conflict, so many times in India.

Shoko and I were sitting outside Lok Nayak Bhavan, the offices of the Home Ministry in Delhi. There was a question about our visa and we had joined the queue waiting for the offices to open. I was next to an Australian whose tourist visa had expired. He asked me what I did. When I told him I taught the Bible he was amazed.

'You must be joking,' he said. 'Religion has caused enough conflict in India. Are you trying to add one more?'

That wasn't what I had said to him. And it certainly wasn't what I thought I was doing. But his question was a serious one. As soon as we talk about spirituality, or about religions, the issue of religious conversion comes up. And that quickly leads to the subject of conflict.

Why? What makes religious conversion such a difficult topic?

Religious conversion is complex and sensitive, because it is a process of change which results in further changes. These can affect both individuals and communities, in all areas of life.

Forced Conversions?

Before we look more closely at these changes, we need to dispose of a distraction. We are *not* talking here about 'forced' conversions. While there are frequent accusations about them, and there are laws to prevent them, documented examples are very few. Where they do happen, it would be very difficult to find any leader from any religion who would approve forced conversions.

A group of Hindus and Christians met recently in Britain to discuss conversion. The first meeting saw all the usual questions, accusations and misperceptions from both sides. Feelings were strong but the group agreed to meet again. Out of the second meeting – somewhat to our surprise – we found ourselves working towards an agreed statement which affirmed '... the importance for both our communities of religious freedom' – to worship, to teach, to change one's faith or to be left alone not to change. The group unanimously repudiated 'strategies for conversion which are coercive or manipulative' and condemned all attacks on places of worship.

When everybody realised that neither side wanted to defend forced conversions, the heat came out of the discussion and we could focus on the real questions: what is happening in conversion? What are the issues that cause division? What are the substantial points of difference, in belief and practice, between people of different faiths?

So we are not talking here about 'forced' conversion.

Yet the reality, as we have already noted several times, is that *any* conversion can be unsettling and disruptive. There can be a variety of motives, factors for choice and further implications, for individuals and communities. Almost all allegations of 'forced' conversion either spring from misunderstanding of these complex issues, or from feelings of hurt and betrayal – or from a sense of threat to vested interests.

Let us look more closely at these issues surrounding

conversion. (The examples I give are from the context of conversion to Christ. But the issues apply to conversion in *any* direction, to or from *any* faith).

1. What is the Connection between the Inner and Outer Aspects of Conversion?

Conversion is an inner experience that has outward effects. Both aspects are important and neglecting either of them leads to distortions. The colonial authorities looked only on the outer aspects, at the converts' legal status and community membership. This created rigid categories, which sometimes made divisions worse. Today some still focus only on these external aspects, while others emphasise the inner and ignore the wider implications.

Conversion involves *inner change*. For example, the good news of Jesus centres around grace, forgiveness, acceptance of persons as they are. When Venkataswami Gupta heard this message it was revolutionary to him. The scriptures in which he had been brought up told him that God comes into the world, in one of his incarnations, to punish the sinners and save the good. But the Christian preachers whom he heard outside his house said that Jesus came into the world to save sinners, not to punish them. He felt liberated from his guilt. Ram Gidoomal heard the same message as a student in the bar at Imperial College, burdened with the load of his *karma*. He also accepted the forgiveness of Christ and committed his life to him. For both, their liberation motivated them to want to bring change to others as well.

For villagers, tribals or slum people whom I have met, Christ was seen as one who liberated by giving acceptance and dignity. He enabled them to overcome habits and attitudes that had enslaved them, or powers that had oppressed them. Their inner spiritual change led to change in other areas, such as attitudes to oneself, to other family members and the world outside.

2. What Are the Wider Effects of Conversion?

But inner changes like these have wider consequences – ethical, cultural, social and political. These may be very positive; certainly the converts hope they will be. But we cannot ignore the potential for the 'socially alienating quality of conversion' (Viswanathan, 1998, p. 85).

Ethical Effects

Ethical effects might include changes in attitudes to the poor, corruption, selfishness, ambition, which would lead to change at a personal and family level. For example, if people's attitude to money and personal pleasure changes, they may begin to work harder, save money instead of wasting it, treat their wives with love instead of downgrading them or beating them. As a result their social and economic situation is likely to change and they may no longer fit into their former society in the same way.

When people are living at a lower level economically or socially, then interventions may be needed at several levels to help transform their situation. For people in the Delhi slums, change begins in their minds and hearts. Spiritual change is basic. But they may also need help in finding work, getting training or learning to read. They may need to learn new patterns of family life, where the husband or father was previously irresponsible or alcoholic. The result of these different interventions may bring quite drastic changes in their way of living.

Sometimes this leads to conflict, for example when people living in slums no longer pay bribes to the slum landlord. Or when low-caste people in the village no longer bow down in abject fear and submission to higher-caste people. Or when tribal people feel, for various reasons, that they cannot join in festivals which their community celebrated before.

Culture and Community

This could be linked to changes of culture and social custom. Christian conversion is a turning from sin to Christ. It is not a turning from culture, family or society. But sometimes this has happened and converts have been encouraged (occasionally even forced) to change their diet, clothes, name, or occupation. Many factors may be involved, with push and pull from different sides. The strength of community in Indian culture can increase the pressure here.

Every culture has good and bad aspects. The person who has found a new faith and allegiance is likely to be critical of some aspects in their culture that he or she sees as bad. In some cases this leads to active rejection of their past. In other cases the person may be willing to stay in the community but faces pressure from the majority, which forces them to leave.

This can be seen as 'changing your religion', in other words leaving your religious and cultural community. The problem here, as we have seen, is disentangling the inner change from the outer structures of community. Conversion to Christ can mean the fulfilment of a person's deepest spiritual longings and access to the One God whom all seek for. It does not have to mean separation from one's community.

Followers of Christ throughout India and the Diaspora wrestle with this issue. They want to demonstrate clear commitment to Christ without losing the good in their culture or being separated from their community.

Each has to work it out in their own situation. Some find they can maintain their links in both directions. In the villages of Andhra Pradesh, the Hindu farmers who began to follow Jesus stayed within their community. Azariah encouraged them to do so, and to retain all aspects of their culture unless they were ethically wrong.

Others find it difficult to identify themselves openly with the Christian church, so they do not take membership or get baptised. Several thousand such 'Non-Baptised Believers in Christ' are reported in Chennai. In Thornton Heath, a suburb of South London, a group of Gujaratis sit on the floor singing *bhajans* at their weekly *satsang*. This *satsang* is dedicated to Jesus and its members are seeking to follow him in different ways. But they are not 'Christians'. They see Christians as a very different community. They want to follow Jesus and remain within their community. How do we describe their spiritual experience? Is it 'conversion'?

Political Effects

In one sense, every conversion is a political act. Gauri Viswanathan compares its impact to 'the forces of modernity ... colonialism ... feminism', because of its appeal to personal choice and action, its introduction of different cultural frameworks, and its 'representation of a subjectivity at variance' with social morality and ritual practice (Viswanathan, 1998, p. 75). In other words, conversion is a powerful force that can provide strong challenges to many areas of social and national life.

This has often been interpreted in a narrow political sense. In the colonial period, or earlier in the Muslim conquests, it was easy for people to link religion with political power, usually the dominant one. People had this perception on either side of the colonial divide. That was especially the case in the pre-Independence period, when political power and representation were closely linked to religion and community. So the 'untouchables' and their relation to the Hindu majority became a political as well as a religious issue.

Conversion to Christ has clear political implications. It is not neutral or merely private. Acknowledging Christ as Lord means acknowledging God's rule and hence the rule of law. This should make Christ's followers the most obedient and conscientious citizens. It also means that elected or appointed (or even hereditary) leaders are ultimately accountable to God for their actions. None of them are above the law or autonomous. So they can and should be called to account.

The freedom and equality of all under law is another sacred gift and responsibility. And because God has given freedom to human beings to choose how they live their lives, his followers must give the same freedom even to those who disagree with them. Christians have not always been good at recognising this, perhaps because of their convictions about truth, or because they confused their institutions with God's Kingdom. But a society that truly follows Christ will be democratic, plural and open.

However, faith in Christ is not linked to any political system or form of government, left, right or centre; monarchy, republic or empire. It does not diminish patriotism. It is certainly not tied to Western culture or Western economic and political systems.

The Western dream – or nightmare?

Christians in the West are struggling today to disentangle those elements of Western culture that have truly been influenced by Christian values over the centuries, from those that have no connection to Christianity or are even opposed to it. They struggle with the materialism and greed that pervade society and are seen in the excesses of unregulated capitalism. This is self-destructive and quite different from the biblical ethic. John Wesley, a spiritual leader and social reformer, told Christians in England to '*earn* all you can, *save* all you can, *give* all you can'. He himself lived on a fixed income and gave away large amounts − because he saw himself as only a steward, not the owner, of the money.

Christians in the West realise that the emphasis on individual freedom, which can be so powerful and liberating, is destructive unless linked to community and concern for the well-being of others. They are distressed by the sexual chaos and breakdown of family life, by inequality and social exclusion, by selfishness and ruthless competition.

They realise that behind many of these tendencies are the rejection of all authority and ultimately the rejection of God, rejections that have profoundly affected European civilisation over the last 400 years.

The social, intellectual and cultural Renaissance in fifteenth and sixteenth century Europe developed into two streams. One was based on the widespread dissemination of the Bible in everyday languages, especially through the printing press. This brought concepts of freedom, equality, personal value and forgiveness, based on the recognition of God as creator and redeemer. The other stream emphasised human reason and the autonomy of the individual. (These concepts are also found in the Bible, but not as absolutes). It increasingly found God irrelevant and in fact offensive. The pioneer scientists and technologists were all people of deep faith in God, whom they acknowledged as the source of their discovery of the principles of nature. But later confidence in the power of science and reason seemed to exclude the necessity of God. Darwin, Freud and Marx were the giants who have changed the way all of us have looked at the world since the mid-nineteenth century.

India does not need to go down that path. Following Christ does not mean uncritically adopting Western ways. On the contrary, it provides moral standards and the personal guidance of Jesus to distinguish good and bad in the bewildering world of modernisation and globalisation.

3. What Are People's Motives in Conversion?

Once again we need to hold together the inner and outer aspects of conversion. We also need to distinguish the perspectives of two different people: the convert or seeker, and the agent of conversion – the preacher, missionary or other religious figure. Often too much attention is given to the latter. There is a lot of discussion about the 'right to convert' (i.e. the right to 'make converts'), assuming that the 'missionary' is the dominant figure, who does something to 'convert' the other.

The Seeker's Motives

Conversion is the act of the person being converted. Christians often speak of 'being converted' because they want to emphasise that this is a spiritual act, in which God is at work. And inner, spiritual change can only be the work of God in their life. There may be a human agent, who conveys the message and may challenge or persuade others. But conversion should be the choice of the person concerned.

What motivates that choice? How free is it? This is where we need to keep firm hold of the inner/outer link. We could say that the initial motive for any conversion is *the desire for change*. That is very broad. It could include social, economic, spiritual, cultural, emotional or psychological change.

What causes the desire for change? It could be dissatisfaction with one's present situation; a personal crisis (sickness, family problems, failure, guilt); exposure to new truth or new values; social or political changes; seeing the possibility of new relationships; responding to love and justice (or the opposite); seeking peace in this life or salvation in the next; questions about the meaning of life; fear of death; protest against injustice or oppression ...

The list could go on. Each of these could be a motive, separately or combined. One may lead to another. Some may begin with concern for well-being in this life and then realise the possibilities in the next life; others might seek eternal salvation and then discover the implications for life in the here-and-now.

In some societies people pursue these concerns as individuals. In others they are accustomed to making decisions and choices as a group – a family or larger community. Both are equally valid, though the expression may vary.

The fact that so many possible motives are listed, and that they may be hard to distinguish, is not accidental. Gauri Viswanathan asks

> Why ... does history throw up so many instances of conversion movements accompanying the fight against racism, sexism, and colonialism? What might be the link between the struggle for basic rights and the adoption of religions typically characterised as minority religions? What limitations of secular ideologies in ensuring these rights do acts of conversion reveal? Does that act of exposure align conversion more closely with cultural criticism? (Viswanathan, 1998, p. xvi)

One answer to her questions is that God made us whole people. We can't neatly separate the different aspects of our lives. We are meant to live fully in this world, but we find

our true identity in a relationship with God that goes beyond
this world.

Converts often face continuing tension. They may have
been pulled by attraction to their new faith and its culture.
Or they may have felt pushed and been critical of their old
faith and culture. Either way, whatever the original
motivation, they may find themselves in a position of
criticism both ways; wanting to reform their old faith and
culture, but equally aware of shortcomings in the new.

Narayan Vaman Tilak, a Brahmin poet in Maharashtra,
became a Christian in the late nineteenth century. While his
passionate commitment to Christ never wavered, he became
very critical of the Christian church and its structures. He
longed to see it more Indian – because he believed that it
could then be a vehicle for a renewed and purged Hinduism.
His ultimate vision was the renewal of India, and he believed
this could only happen through a deep religious awakening,
centred on Jesus as the true Guru:

> Thrice blessed is thy womb, my motherland,
> Whence mighty *rishis*, saints and sages spring!
> A Christian I, yet here none taunteth me,
> Nor buffeteth with angry questioning.
> My Guru they delight to venerate; they say,
> 'He is our brother and our kin.'

Being in between can be stimulating, but it is usually
uncomfortable. Dr B. R. Ambedkar announced his intention
to leave Hinduism over twenty years before he actually did
so. During that time he was moving back and forth between
the Hindu culture which he was so critical of, and the various
possibilities for change that lay ahead. His final choice was
Buddhism, which he carefully studied and wrote about. But
the Neo-Buddhism he expounded was in a real sense his own
reformed version, incorporating his own deepest values.

Missionary Motives

What are the motives of the 'missionary', the person who is seeking to share his or her beliefs with others? These are usually clearer, in theory, until they encounter the complexity of human response that we have seen.

Ebe Sunder Raj explains it like this:

> If Christ's life and sayings be the ultimate truth for a disciple of Christ, he can with all humility invite others, with neither apology nor arrogance, to come further up from where they stand, to see his Guru as the ultimate Truth. (*National Debate on Conversion*, Bharat Jyoti, 2001, p. 6)

The focus is on teaching truth, with ultimate, other-worldly implications. Why then do so many Christian 'missionaries' spend so much time and effort in social services, caring for people's material, this-worldly needs? Is this a distraction? Or is it, as often alleged, simply a cover, a 'sweetener', an inducement, exploitation?

This is the commonest allegation and the one that is hardest to dispel. But the explanation is very simple. It is the fact to which we have frequently referred: that God made us whole people, in whom the spiritual, physical, social, intellectual, emotional, individual and corporate are all dimensions of the one person.

> The more I attain to Thee, so much the more do I desire Thee. Such is the state of my heart, O Lord.

Narayan Vaman Tilak's words express the spiritual desire for God which is the centre of our lives. But they don't exclude the reality of God's concern for the rest of our lives, with which God is also concerned. We have seen this illustrated in all the stories in this book.

For the modern person, with a materialist mindset, this holistic perspective is strictly meaningless. The spiritual is a private and individual value, without objective foundation. Some Christians fall into this mindset. They over-emphasise the material, this-worldly dimension and omit the need to call people back to God.

Some religious and political leaders take the opposite view. They argue that any social concern has to be a 'cover' for the real agenda, which is 'conversion'. But what does that mean? Speaking like that ignores the reality of life and reduces 'conversion' to a single dimension, whereas we have seen that it has many dimensions. Such people cannot, or will not, see that there need not be any contradiction between serving people's immediate needs (and so demonstrating the reality of God's concern), and also going beyond it to their ultimate, eternal condition. Some Christians also fail to see this connection and are tempted to downplay social concern or see it only as a means to an end.

All the friends whose stories I have told here are examples of people who serve others as whole people.

Conclusion

Conversion is a complex change, because any intervention in people's lives, whether external or internal, brings change, at different levels, inner and outer. It is one of the many sources of change, positive and negative, in Indian society today.

People focus on religious conversion as a major source of disruption. But any social changes can be difficult. M. C. Mathew points out that many in India have enormous economic and social opportunities: 'If you have the resources you can have what you want.' But even more face a growing gap that leaves them marginalised and frustrated. 'When this kind of alienation and stratification increase, we can't predict the outcome.' But we can see the caste wars in Bihar, the

Chilikh Prawn Riots in Orissa, or the agitations against globalisation or building dams. These are the result of social conflict, without any element of 'religious conversion'.

But we still haven't answered the question: why do we need conversion at all?

14
Changing India: What is the Goal?

Wealth is evidently not the good we are seeking; for it is merely useful and for the sake of something else.
— *Aristotle*

Constitutions... may channel men's actions and prescribe limits for political actions, but they cannot reform or improve human character.
— *Granville Austin*

Isn't all this talk about conversion unnecessary? Shouldn't we rather help each other to a better understanding and practice of the faith that each of us has inherited? Isn't education a better way to bring change, without bringing in religious beliefs or emphasising differences? If we encourage others to change their beliefs, isn't that exclusive and arrogant? To claim that you have the truth seems to imply that others are wrong and in some way inferior.

We need to step back a bit and examine two ways of looking at religion. That will also help us in our basic question: how do we decide the direction in which we want to change – for ourselves, for our community, for India?

One View of Religion

According to one view, you are *born* into your religion. Religion, culture, community, country are all closely linked. Gandhiji said that 'Every *nation* considers its own faith to be as good as that of any other ... Certainly the great faiths held by *the people of India* are adequate *for her people.*' Notice the words I have italicised. In other words, different parts of the world will follow different religious paths, which are most suitable to them. On this basis many assume that the West is 'Christian' while the Middle East is Muslim, South Asia is Hindu, Sikh or Muslim, and so on. (In the same way, Samuel Huntington's *The Clash of Civilisations* divides the world into religious-cultural blocs, which will compete with each other, now that the Cold War is over. The World Trade Center bombing and its aftermath have shown all too clearly the effects of this approach. The 'clash' is in danger of becoming a self-fulfilling prophecy, based on an over-simplifying analysis.)

Underlying this is the deeply held conviction that the different manifestations of belief and practice are only that – they are simply outward expressions of an underlying universal spiritual reality. It may be called by different names, but it is the same, ultimate source of all spiritual energy. Every region or culture has its own way to God, and they are all valid. There is no point in fighting over apparent differences. And there is no point in changing from the religion into which you were born; this only creates tension and disloyalty.

This is a geographical, cultural, community approach to religion. Truth depends on where you are and who you are. On this understanding, there is no valid place for conversion.

This view is attractive. But it doesn't fully answer two questions:

- How do we choose between different – sometimes opposing – values within the different religions and cultures?
- What is the basic problem facing human beings?

A Vision for India

Let me try to illustrate by giving my own vision for India. This is what I would like to see India become.

India is so big, so varied, so rich in every way. From the Kanyakumari fisherman, to the teenage computer millionaire, to the daily labourer in Bihar, to the Bollywood screen goddess, to the fighter pilot in the Western desert, it's all one country.

- **I would like to see an India in which each person has equal dignity and value, yet keeps his or her diversity and unique culture and community ties.**

What will be the basis for this? It cannot be culture, religion or community alone. That becomes divisive, as we can see in the example of Pakistan. Or in the complaint of 'FPJ', writing in *Asian Voice* (a London weekly) about:

> ... a massive non-Hindu population that expects rights and privileges not available to Hindus. Just consider the Ayodhya issue. Hindus cannot build a *mandir* in their own country ... India should declare itself 'The Hindu Republic of India', a country which Hindus can feel proud of ... The caste system is divisive and indefensible ... all Hindus are equal. (*Asian Voice*, 4 March 2000)

S. S. Gill comments:

> God seems to have taken special care to make India ungovernable. Her extreme diversities and disparities make the emergence of large common denominators almost impossible. Our much flaunted unity in diversity has a very narrow base ... Thus it becomes extremely difficult to evolve common codes of behaviour and conduct ... In our society there is caste ethics and there

are group norms, but there is no such thing as Indian social norms. (Gill, 1998, pp. 251, 253)

The Biblical basis would be the equality of all citizens – whatever their beliefs or community – created by God, under the God-given rule of law, but also created differently, set in different families, communities and people groups and so free to follow their own beliefs and practices, within that framework of God's law.

• **I would like to see an India in which individuals are free to choose their direction in life, yet still recognise their place in their family and community.**

That sentence asks a lot. It implies that they have an understanding of different opportunities in life *(basic education for all)*; that they can expect to live a reasonably healthy life *(basic health care for all)*; that that they have enough income to live on *(access to work and to credit)*; that they are not just dependent on or obligated to others *(fair distribution of land and resources; opportunities for private enterprise and initiative; markets based on fairness, not just freedom)*. All this – and at the same time keeping their responsibility to other members of their family, older and younger.

It implies a commitment to justice and energetic enterprise, with a belief in both individual *and* community.

How do we balance all these requirements? The usual answer is to rely on family and community. In other words, we each look after 'our own people'. Surely that is the best way, if we all follow it? But what about others, especially those who are weak?

• **I would like to see an India in which the stronger groups and communities are concerned for the interests of other groups who are not related to them, and especially for the weaker and marginalised.**

That isn't always easy. In the 1970s the Doordarshan TV channel tried, in its old-fashioned way, to protect its viewers (the weaker members of society?) from the harmful influence of what it considered 'lighter culture'. It promoted educational and uplifting TV programmes and tried to keep out the trivial. The aim was good, but the result was a stifling lack of creativity. Now market forces have come in with their brutal approach, leaving some looking back with nostalgia to the good old days.

It's a real issue, and the usual approach of looking after 'our own people' is inadequate. Orissa's Kalahandi District, once a hopeless 'basket case', is hailed as a success story because of its dramatic transformation through irrigation. But who benefits there? It seems that only the rich do. 'Looking after our own people' leads to caste politics and caste wars.

The Old Testament book of Deuteronomy speaks of the duty of caring for the weak and marginalised, because God 'shows no partiality and takes no bribes. He defends the cause of the fatherless and the widow and loves the alien, giving him food and clothing. And you are to love those who are aliens' (The Old Testament, Deuteronomy 10.17-19).

- **I would like to see an India in which the spiritual and the material are both recognised as important.**

God made us whole people. We don't have to choose between escaping from the material world for spiritual experience, or abandoning God and ethics in the pursuit of wealth.

Well, my vision may not contain many surprises. It may look very idealistic. Or it may look familiar: the Constitution of India is based on very similar ideals. But if we were to adopt it, we would need to make some hard choices. As Granville Austin points out, the Constitution gives the ideal, but we have to be changed in order to fulfil it. And we would need to find a basis on which these ideals could actually be practised.

Which Way is India Going?

Commentators generally offer one of two predictions for India. One is optimistic and up-beat. India's ancient wisdom, her modern technology, above all the ability of her people, all point to a bright future, in a world that finally recognises India's contribution. ' "Wake up O India, thy time has come!" Vivekananda's call is repeated today.' (Francois Gautier, *Asian Voice*, 11 March 2000).

The other side focuses on the rising tide of corruption and criminality. President K. R. Narayanan, addressing the nation on the eve of Independence Day (14 August 2000) referred to 'poverty, ignorance, disease and superstition ... the growth of violence ... the encircling gloom of these negative tendencies'. He went on to speak of other 'positive and encouraging trends that give hope to us'.

S. S. Gill describes corruption as a cancer at the heart of India. Against those who take a functional view of corruption as an economic lubricant, he points out the 'havoc' that corruption wreaks. It spreads inefficiency; widens the gap between rich and poor; creates negligence in administration; drains time and energy; increases accidents; distorts the value of honest work; makes a mockery of planning; subverts egalitarian goals; hits at values such as public morality, social justice, communal harmony, law and order. (Gill, 1998, pp. 266-268)

Who is right? Which scenario is accurate? The weakness of many analyses, including my description above (and many similar and much better expressed visions), is that they don't explicitly acknowledge the real problem that prevents us from fulfilling our potential.

The problem is not that these visions are irrelevant. They actually sum up the longings of most of humanity, not just

Indians. There *should* be a way in which we can live together in harmony and equity. The problem that is not mentioned is the problem of evil.

The Intractable Problem of Evil

We actually know the right way forward, as Sam Pitroda pointed out in his London lecture. We have the resources, with India's vast natural and above all human wealth, to provide for everybody. We have the best brains, the best business skills, the most diverse and adaptable labour force, the richest family and community tradition. Then why do we face such terrible social divisions, such a gap between rich and poor, a crippling defence budget, incurable hostility with neighbours? Why is there such corruption and greed, so much selfish ambition? Why are family relations breaking down, between the generations, between husband and wife?

We can give a range of explanations: social, economic, cultural and historical. They are all valid as far as they go. But at the bottom is the intractable problem of evil in human nature. We know what is good but we don't do it. We know what is wrong but we still do it. As S. S. Gill reminds us, 'in India all of us have a stake in corruption' (Gill, 1998, p. 261).

The Human Paradox

This, of course, is not India's problem; it is the human problem.

The Bible's analysis is radical. Its view of human nature is both extremely optimistic and extremely pessimistic. Human beings are made by God. So we each have unique dignity and value. We were created as individuals but to live in community. And our highest destiny is to live in relationship with God, living out his purpose in our world.

In that relationship our potential is limitless. 'The glory of God is a human being fully alive', said an early Christian teacher, Irenaeus.

But the other side of the story is that human beings have rejected this relationship and preferred to go their own way, without acknowledging God's direction. The Bible calls this 'sin' and says that this is the cause of the alienation we experience – from ourselves, from each other, from the world of nature, and ultimately from God. The beautiful design has been fatally spoiled. 'All are basically gentle,' says the Dalai Lama. But that is only half the story.

That is why we can't get on with each other. We need first to turn back to God, our Creator, and acknowledge him. Our problem is not just ignorance. It's our rebellion against God.

Is there any solution? That brings us to another way of looking at religion.

Another View of Religion

This is the view expressed by Paul, one of Jesus' early followers, to the intellectual elders of Athens, the cultural capital of the Mediterranean world (The New Testament, Acts 17.22-34). He was asked to give an explanation of his preaching about Jesus.

It is true, Paul said, that people have been seeking God in their different ways and places. Their images and ideas represent their yearning for God. And God has revealed himself, to some extent, to everybody. Everybody knows God as the creator and the source of our being, though he is much greater than our imagining. So all of us are equal as human beings, equally subject to God's law, equally responsible for each other. We know this but don't follow it in practice.

So at a certain point in history God intervened and

actually became part of our world, as a human being – Jesus. That became the decisive turning point. It was not just us seeking God, but God seeking us. And it provided the standard by which all of us can judge how far our efforts to seek God have been authentic.

The fact is that not all of us have been equally sincere. Some of us have been quite insincere. We have made our own choices about how things should be and how God should act. And we have often failed to do even what we thought was the right thing to do. Jesus came into the world to show people the truth – supremely about God's love and forgiveness. But he also came to judge us for our untruth. Our problem is not just about knowing who or what to believe. We lack the moral and spiritual power to practise what we do know.

S. S. Gill concludes his hard-hitting and pessimistic analysis of corruption on a slight note of hope:

> I place my bet on empowerment of the people and a transparent government for a decisive turnaround. (Gill, 1998, p. 270)

We, the people, have to change – and if we can, there is hope. But who will change us?

When we understand this problem, we begin to understand the significance of Jesus' coming. We need a mediator – somebody to represent both God and humanity; to offer forgiveness; to give the power to change from sin and evil; to overcome death. Only Jesus offers this, through his life, death and resurrection. That is why he is the universal saviour, not because one 'religion' is better than another.

Jesus also provides a personal approach to God. God's law and justice are fundamental. But they are principles, which can be abstract. Gandhiji could say 'Truth is God' and have the strength of will to follow the principle. But M.C.

Mathew found that 'what was not sufficient was that there was no spontaneous inner momentum in those who became part of his political system, because they had no personal encounter with a personal God.'

We need more than principles; we need a personal being to whom we can relate, one who inspires and empowers us. Ken Gnanakan spoke of Jesus as one who embodies *krupa*, 'grace', and is accessible both to the marginalised and to the rich and privileged. He suffered himself and so he identifies with those who suffer, and shows that God cares.

'Why can't you just do your good works, care for those in need? Do you need to talk about Christ as well?' asked my friend.

But you can't have one without the other. Christ is the inspiration and his love and forgiveness provide the power to change. That is why Christians serve people and invite them to turn to Christ. Not to exploit them or pressurise them – but because they believe this is the best they can offer. Talk to Azariah, Arole, MC and Anna, Iris, Ken, Ram, Vinod and many others – you will get the same answer. Their service is unconditional. But it is inescapably based on their commitment to Christ.

Conversion for All

This view of religion is radically different. It distinguishes spiritual reality from culture, community and geography. On this understanding, we *all* need conversion – not from one 'religion' to another but from sin and self towards God. It is not our religion, or our parents' religion, but our relationship with God and our response to Christ, which matter.

William Carey was an educationist, missionary, social reformer and entrepreneur who made a profound contribution to India in the early nineteenth century. Several years after arriving in India, he baptised Krishna Pal, the first Hindu to be 'converted' through his preaching. On the same occasion Carey baptised his own son Felix, a young adult who also needed 'conversion' – not from another religion but from his basic sin to God. Both Krishna Pal and Felix needed a new life through Christ.

Freedom to Choose

Conversion to Christ is a radical change. Those who have followed Christ believe it is the most significant change in any person's life. Others may or may not agree. It is vital that we allow each other the freedom to change – or not to change – in any direction we choose.

Of course, the freedom to choose the changes we would like is a luxury in today's world. Outside forces are constantly impinging on our lives. The Planning Commission in Delhi decides to build a new dam. A multinational company enters a joint agreement with an Indian business to open a new factory. The lives of thousands – probably millions – of villagers are irrevocably changed at a stroke. The manufacture of private vehicles is liberalised and millions of city people are doomed to increasing pollution and ill health. The greed of traders and government officials together results in unfair distribution and millions more are kept in poverty.

Despite this, freedom of choice is precious. We need to keep on struggling for it.

It is important also to recognise that the choices we make will lead in different directions. Our worldview affects the way that we think and live. Hari Lal, a high official in a government undertaking, invited a Christian friend to bring a medical team to his village in Uttar Pradesh.

'Why is it', he asked his driver, a Jain, 'that the Christians are willing to come? I have tried to get other doctors but they don't want to come to the rural areas.'

'Perhaps it's because the Christians believe they have only one life', came the driver's immediate reply.

Whatever he meant, your view of God and of the world does make a practical difference. I sat with a close friend from university days, now a senior government official in Delhi with an exemplary record of public service. His daughter was about to get married and she was telling us, full of enthusiasm, about her recent renewal of spiritual experience and understanding, through a combination of following a guru, insights from psychology and her desire to serve others. We were reflecting on different religious experiences. What did we have in common? What were the differences? What about the claims of different religious leaders?

'Ultimately all religions involve surrender', said my friend. *'You surrender your will to God. But it does make a difference who you surrender to.'*

Precisely. The one you surrender to may offer different promises, make different demands, lead in different directions. We need to choose.

For Further Reading

The following are books quoted in the text, and a very brief selection of others of interest.

The Debate about Conversion

Arun Shourie has been the chief recent critic of Christian missionary work in India, in: *Missionaries in India*, ASA Publications, 1994; Rupa, 2001; *Harvesting Our Souls*, ASA Publications, 2000; Rupa, 2001.

Ashok Chowgule has also summarised many of the questions raised in: *Christianity in India: The Hindutva Perspective*, Hindu Vivek Kendra, 1999. Two of the main respondents are:

Vishal Mangalwadi, *Missionary Conspiracy*, Nivedit Good Books, 1996.

Ebe Sunder Raj, *National Debate on Conversion*, Bharat Jyoti, 2001, and *Divide and Rule*, Bharat Jyoti, 1999.

Key Books on Conversion

Andrew Wingate, *The Church and Conversion*, ISPCK, 1997.

Gauri Viswanathan, *Outside the Fold: Conversion, Modernity and Belief*, Princeton University Press, 1998.

William Oddie, *Hindu and Christian in South-East India*, Curzon Press, 1991.

Social Protest in India, Manohar, 1979.

Religion in South Asia: Religious Conversion and Revival Movements in South Asia in Medieval and *Modern Times*, South Asia Books, 1977; Manohar 1991.

Other Books

Beulah Wood & Lalitha Chellappa, *Pioneering on the Pinda: The Story of RAC Paul and Iris Paul,* ELS, Chennai, 1998.

Brijraj Singh, *Ziegenbalg: The First Protestant Missionary to India,* Oxford University Press, 1999.

C. J. Fuller, *Caste Today,* Oxford University Press, 1997.

Daniel O'Connor, *Din-Sevak: Verrier Elwin's Life of Service in Tribal India,* ISPCK, 1993.

Joy Pachuau, *Assessment of the Socio-Cultural, Political, Religious and Economic Developments in the North East in Post-Independence India,* Unpublished paper, New Delhi, 1999.

Ken Gnanakan, *Still Learning,* ACTS Trust, 1991.

Katherine Makower, *Beginnings: The Story of the Special Children at Ashirvad,* Christian Medical College & Hosptal, Vellore, 1998.

Lakshmibai Tilak, *I Follow After: An Autobiography,* Oxford University Press, 1950 and 1998.

Lalchungnunga, *Mizoram: Politics of Regionalism and National Integration,* Reliance Publishing House, 1994.

Meera Kosambi (ed.), *Pandita Ramabai through Her Own Words,* Oxford University Press, 2000.

Moddie, A.D., *Men of Straw,* Harper Collins, 1997.

Ravi Tiwari, *Yesudas: The Witness of a Convert,* ISPCK, 2000.

Samuel Jeyakumar, *Dalit Consciousness and Christian Conversion,* ISPCK, 1999.

S. S. Gill, *The Pathology of Corruption,* Harper Collins, 1998.

Vishal Mangalwadi & Nicol McNicol, *A Tribute to an Indian Woman: The Life of Pandita Ramabai,* Nivedit Good Books, 1996.